'Of Variegated Hues':
The Poetry and Translations
of
A.K. Ramanujan

'Of Variegated Hues': The Poetry and Translations of A.K. Ramanujan

RAMA NAIR

PRESTIGE

Prestige Books
3/28, East Patel Nagar
New Delhi 110 008

ISBN: 81-7551-119-2

Printed at Chaman Offset Press, New Delhi 110 002

Contents

For
Sahadev
Jaya
Gita

Preface

My interest in A.K. Ramanujan began in 1975 when I was a post-graduate student at Arts College, Osmania University, Hyderabad. Over the years, this interest developed into admiration and fascination for the works of this immensely talented and creative writer. A monograph on his poetry in 1976 was followed by numerous talks and papers that were delivered and published over the last two decades. In 1998-99, the grant of a Minor U.G.C. Research Project enabled me to continue research on "A Comparative Study of the Poetry and Translations of A.K. Ramanujan." The successful completion of this project in March 1999 was the final driving force that motivated me to undertake the task of writing this book.

The greater part of my thanks, as usual, goes to Prof. M. Sivaramkrishna, Head (Retd) of the Department of English, Osmania University, Hyderabad for his invaluable guidance and help at all times.

Thanks are also due to Prof. C.D. Narasimhaiah for his generosity in permitting me to use the library at 'Dhvanyaloka,' Mysore, and for his gracious hospitality while I was there.

I also take this opportunity to thank all my friends, and colleagues in the Department of English, Osmania University, Hyderabad, for their encouragement and support.

Finally, my special thanks go to Dr. R.K. Dhawan of Prestige Books for his faith in the validity and relevance of this book, and for his ready acceptance to publish it.

Osmania University
Hyderabad

RAMA NAIR

Chapter I

The Birth and Development of Indian English Verse

The literary scene in India is the amalgam of a number of cultures, traditions, languages, and ideological perspectives. To isolate any one from the mainstream calls for perseverance, fortitude, and a careful assessment of the existing literary tradition. India, before the advent of the British, had been a fascinating country of the exotic East. For centuries it had been occupied with the study of oriental learning alone. The mystical veil which enshrouded India was pulled aside with the establishment of British trade in India. One step led to another, and with its firm hold on the trade in India, the British soon established their supremacy over Indian affairs.

British rule in India began with Clive's victory in the Battle of Plassey in 1757. This led to the establishment of the British Empire in India, and India itself, from a proud country with an enviable cultural and literary background degenerated into one of Imperial Britain's many exploited and subjugated colonies. The effects of colonialism were felt in all aspects of Indian life—the political, social, and cultural. But the worst was yet to come. Indian Independence in 1947 from the British did not mitigate the baneful effects of colonialism. It clung like an evil shroud over the intellect of the new generation of post-Independence India, breeding a unique phenomena called neo-colonialism—its most powerful weapon being the unabated use of English, the language of the British in India.

However, English as a popular language gained currency with the arrival of the Christian missionaries in India in the nineteenth century. The Evangelical Movement in England created an ardour for reform and religious conversion. Missionaries were permitted to propagate their religion in India, and the mode they used to do so was to convert the Indians by educating and reforming them. No means was considered too foul. It was a ruthless and calculated tactic to undermine and destroy the culture and tradition of an ancient civilization. The extent of the calumny indulged in by them took on monstrous proportions. "If all India stands up," Swami Vivekananda told the Christians in America about the propaganda, "and takes all the mud that is at the bottom of the Indian Ocean and throws it up against the Western countries, it will not be doing an infinitesimal part of what you are doing to us."[1] Swami Vivekananda further stated that he was not hostile to the Christian missionaries in India, but only to the viciousness of their distortions and misrepresentations of the religion in India. The process of proselytizing was carried on with the unavoidable task of educating the 'natives' in the English language. The object was to teach the Indians English, and through that to open their minds to modern, Western learning. But there was a controversy between the "Orientalists"—that is, those who exhorted that the natives be instructed in their own languages, and such books as were venerated and revered in their country—and those who urged that they be taught English, and through that, Western values and learning. This created certain problematic issues. Charles Edward Trevelyan, a young civil servant, raised them in a tract, *On the Education of the People of India*, which received sufficient acclaim at the time. The questions addressed were whether an Indian "should be taught at all? Would it not be safer to leave them to wallow in ignorance and ritual and superstition? Would education not ignite ideas of freedom and the rest?"[2] Only two ideals mattered to Britain—of converting India to Christianity, and of securing the Empire for Britain. To do this there had to be a clearly defined object—and it was here that Macaulay's famous *Minute* of 1835 was declared to form "a class of persons, Indians in blood and colour, but English in taste, in opinions, in morals, and in intellect."[3] It asserted those notorious prejudices which flourish to this day among the so-called educated urban elite of

India—the worthlessness of everything Indian, and the infinite superiority of everything British. On 7 March, 1835, Lord William Bentick declared that "the great object of the British Government ought to be the promotion of European literature and science among the natives of India."[4] Macaulay's *Minute* of 1835 became the official policy. Four years later he revelled in the effects of English education in India. He wrote to his father that "Our English classes are flourishing wonderfully. We find it difficult—indeed, in some places impossible—to provide instruction for all who want it. . . . The effect of this education on the Hindoos is prodigious. . . . It is my firm belief that, if our plans of education are followed up, there will not be a single idolator among the respectable classes in Bengal thirty years hence. And this will be effected without any effort to proselytise; without the smallest interference with religious liberty; merely by the natural operation of knowledge and reflection. I heartily rejoice in the prospect."[5]

English education for the Indians was reserved for the equally important secondary task of creating a "second class" cadre of 'babus' or clerks who would man the onerous administrative machinery of the British political power in India. Macaulay's *Minute* converted English to the status of the official language of India. With this began the anglicization of the educated classes. To many 'progressive minded' Indians, the English language stood as the magic door to enlightenment, culture, and art. A number of educational institutions were opened to impart knowledge about English to those Indians who were desirous of learning it.

The entire Indian scene underwent a radical change. A revolutionary transformation took place in the field of learning. The most important amongst these educational institutions was the Hindu College of Calcutta, which later came to be known as the Presidency College. It was chiefly responsible for cultivating a taste for the English language and literature among the Indians. The learning of European literature was encouraged, and thus, the foundation of the English language was laid in India. Indians writing in English became the new phenomenon in the nineteenth century.

This body of writing has been termed variously as Indo-Anglian literature, Anglo-Indian literature, Indo-English literature, and Indian writing in English. Indian English literature may be defined as literature written originally in English by authors Indian by birth, ancestry or nationality. Neither Anglo-Indian literature nor the other literatures can be a part of this literature. The former comprises the writings of British or Western authors concerning India. Rudyard Kipling, E.M. Forster, F.W. Bain, Sir Edwin Arnold, F.A. Steel, John Masters, Paul Scott, M.M. Kaye and many others wrote about India. But their writings would come under British literature. Translations from the Indian languages into English cannot form part of Indian English literature except when the authors themselves undertake creative translations in their work. Indian English literature is not a part of English literature, nor is it a part of Indian literature. In 1962, K.R. Srinivasa Iyengar used the phrase 'Indian Writing in English' for his first exhaustive study of the work. The Sahitya Akademi subsequently accepted the term 'Indian English literature' as the most appropriate designation for this body of writing. M.K. Naik points out that this term emphasizes two significant ideas. "First that this literature constitutes one of the many streams that join the great ocean called Indian literature, which, though written in different languages, has an unmistakable unity: and secondly, that it is an inevitable product of nativization of the English language to express the Indian sensibility."[6]

The modernization process started in the eighteenth century in India. The emergence of Indian English literature was an aspect of the Renaissance. Some officials of the East India Company were scholars with a deep interest in oriental culture. The spread of English education and Western ideas was imbibed earnestly by young Indians to whom it stood as a passport to a newer and a more promising world of liberal values and ideas. The cause of English education was further propagated by Raja Ram Mohan Roy. In the *Letter on English Education* addressed to the Governor-General, Lord Amherst in 1823, he spoke persuasively against the establishment of a Sanskrit school in preference to one imparting English education. While "the Sanskrit system of education would be best calculated to keep this country in darkness," English education would lead to "the improvement of the native population" and "it will consequently promote a more liberal and enlightened system of instruction."[7]

With the popularity of the English language on the rise, the 'new' Indian intellectuals obviously felt the desire to articulate their experience of human situations, human concerns and the depth, variety, and reality of human life in their newly acquired language. Poetry, prose, fiction and drama were the literary genres they employed to express their state of awareness.

Early Indo-Anglian poetry was confined to the social circles of the British residents in India. In a society reeking of personal jealousies, intrigues, and amorous affairs, poetry found its natural outlet in lampoons, satires and epigrams. For instance, there were grand dinners at which English ladies cast their modesty aside, and gluttonously ate their way through the numerous courses that were prepared every night in imitation of the native Muslim aristocracy. 'Quiz,' an anonymous writer, satirised them when he wrote:

> March to the barracks where with joy
> Their masticators they employ,
> On curry, rice and beef and goat,
> Voraciously they cram each throat.[8]

Besides, the arrival of shiploads of unmarried British women in Calcutta in search of rich husbands caused the composition of numerous ironical Verses. These women employed all means to look attractive, but the result as one satirist in 1813 put it, was:

> Pale faded stuffs, by time grown faint
> Will brighten up through art
> A Britain gives their faces paint,
> For sale at India's mart.[9]

Contemporary events excited much of the poetry then. Though the quality was inferior, it nevertheless aroused much interest, and became highly popular.

The gamut of early Indo-Anglian poetry was not entirely satirical. There emerged a set of highly intellectual Englishmen who changed the trend of Indo-Anglian poetry. The quality of the literary output increased. Indian Art and Thought interested them. The writing of William Jones reveals the depth of his knowledge regarding the Indian lore, and the Upanishads, and his 'Ode to Narayana' is worthy of note. The earliest book of Verse in English by an Indian was probably written in 1825. It was Cavelly Venkata Ramaswami's English rendering of a seventeenth century Sanskrit poem 'Viswaguna-darsana' of Arasanipala Venkatadhvarin. But since it is a translation it cannot legitimately form a part of Indian English literature.

The actual history of Indian English poetry commenced with Henry L. Derozio (1809-1831). It was he who inspired a number of young Indians with a love for the English language and its literature. His zeal was such that the orthodox Hindu society in Calcutta took umbrage at his critical stance towards Hindu religious practices and political issues. In 1831 he was expelled for his 'subversive' behaviour from the Hindu College where he had taught for several years. In a poem dedicated to his pupils here, he writes:

> Expanding like the petals of young flowers
> I watch the gentle opening of your minds,

And later he continues in the same poem:

> What joyance rains upon me when I see
> Fame in the mirror of futurity,
> Weaving the chaplets you have yet to gain,
> Ah then I feel I have not lived in vain.[10]

In his brief poetic career, he published two volumes of poetry: *Poems* (1827) and *The Fakeer of Jungheera*: *A Metrical Tale and Other Poems* (1828). His shorter poems were influenced by the British Romantics, while his satirical verses show the influence of Byron. Derozio, in spite of his passion for the English language and English education was a staunch patriot. Poems like 'To India—My Native Land,' 'The Harp of India' and 'To the Pupils of Hindu College' mark him as a true Indian English poet. He was also among the first Indian poets in English to use Indian myth and legend, imagery and diction.

Derozio was followed by Kasiprasad Ghose (1809-1873), the first Indian (Derozio being partly Portuguese) to write verses in English. Several of his verses were collected in *The Shair*, or *Minstrel* (1830). His poetry is imitative of the poetry of Sir Walter Scott. Kasiprasad Ghose had no real originality, his poetry abounding in conventional descriptions and prosaic moralizings. The poem 'To a Young Hindu Widow' exemplifies this:

> Ah, fair one! lone as a desert flower
> Whose bloom and beauty are in vain;
> How dark was that too fatal hour
> Which brought thee lasting grief and pain.[11]

He was followed by other Indian English poets like Gooroo Churun Dutt, Raj Narain Dutt, Michael Madhusudan Dutt, and Shoshee Chunder Dutt, all of whom gained prominence in the second quarter of the nineteenth century.

Michael Madhusudan Dutt (1824-73) was a noteworthy writer in Bengali. But he wrote sonnets and short verses in English besides writing two long poems in English entitled *The Captive Ladie* (1849), and *Visions of the Past* (1849). *Visions of the Past* was a poor imitation of Milton's *Paradise Lost*. Though an accomplished verse writer, his poems remained derivative and inferior.

The first period of Indian English literature ended in the 1850s, a few years before the Indian Revolt of 1857. The shift in attitude is evident in the writings that follow. While English had been accepted favourably by most Indians before the Revolt, the Indian Revolt of 1857 brought about a different set of attitudes and stances. These changes held the potential of bringing about an authentic artistic expression instead of the imitative and derivative verses that had been written earlier.

Early Indian English Poetry was influenced to a large extent by the Romanticism of Byron, Scott, Wordsworth and Shelley. The first notable work in poetry after 1857 was evident in *The Dutt Family Album* (1876). The only example of family anthology in Indian English poetry, it is a collection of 187 poems by the three Dutt brothers—Govin Chunder, Hur Chunder, Greece Chunder, and their cousin, Omesh Chunder. Though technically competent, they did not possess any authenticity of artistic thought or creative response.

It was with Toru Dutt (1856-77) that Indian poetry in English began to have a tone of authenticity. Toru Dutt's Calcutta surroundings greatly inspired her poetic faculties. Her poems were generally lyrical, and she also wrote ballads on legendary historical themes. The glorification of heroic deeds and domestic virtues also appealed to her brother R.C. Dutt, who wrote poems in the same tradition. Toru Dutt's 'Our Casaurina Tree' is an example of her narrative and lyrical excellence. The theme is entirely Indian, and in it she expressed her joys and sorrows. The tree is a symbol of time and eternity, and she prays "May Love defend thee from oblivion's curse." Under its boughs she had played with her brother and sister "Who now in blessed sleep for aye repose."[12] The Casaurina is dear to her soul for it brings back the happy memories of her childhood with such force that the hot tears blind her eyes. Though brought up in Europe, Toru was an Indian at heart and her poems reveal the innate love she had for Nature. The Hindu element is apparent in most of her poems as in 'Savitri.' An impressive feature of her poetry was the absence of any kind of imitation of the Western poets.

In the last quarter of the nineteenth century, genuine lyric poetry and lyrical narrative poetry occupied a position of its own. Manmohan Ghose was another poet who was active during this period. He was sent to England at an early age. His studies of the Elizabethans and older English lyricists, and Greek poetry greatly influenced his own poetry. He was a writer of lyrics, and a group of poems entitled 'Immortal Eve' and 'Orphic Mysteries' reveal the deep love he had for his invalid wife, and the feeling of loneliness that overtook him after her death.

Swami Vivekananda, Sarojini Naidu and Rabindranath Tagore were the other writers of this period. They represent the best of Indian English verse in its philosophical aspect. Sri Aurobindo and Sarojini Naidu, who spent their impressionable years in England when the 'Decadent' poets dominated the scene, reveal the influence of this trend in their early poems. For sheer romanticism, Sarojini Naidu's poems have no parallel in Indian English verse. The introduction of Indian themes gave a new vitality to her poetry. Her poems abound in glittering phrases which dazzle the reader with their descriptive beauty. In 'Palanquin Bearers' she describes the young bride in the following way,

> She sways like a flower in the wind, of our song
> She skims like a bird on the foam of a stream
> She floats like a laugh from the lips of a dream.
> Gaily, O gaily we glide and we sing,
> We bear her along like a pearl on a string.[13]

Sri Aurobindo, and Tagore with his poems in Bengali, together with Sarojini Naidu, and to a certain extent, Toru Dutt, helped to build the image of the Indian English poet. The Indian English poets were bound together by the love they had for India, their motherland. The Indian English poet believed in spirituality as the primary note of Indian life, whether he gave only an occasional expression to it like Sarojini Naidu, or was steeped in it like Sri Aurobindo. For his theme, the Indian English poet drew liberally from Indian myth, legend and history. Early Indian English poetry like the rest of modern Indian English poetry, is Indian first, and everything else afterwards. The last quarter of the nineteenth century may be said to be the golden period of early Indian English poetry.

Indian English poetry is the product of the impact of two cultures, Indian and British. It is the result of the meeting between the East and the West. The English language established itself in India when social development in India had not gained much ground. The impact of modern literary forms on Indians was tremendous. It brought about an entire change in their thinking. The intellectuals busied themselves absorbing and assimilating the new consciousness and the new literary forms for nearly a century. It was thus inevitable that the English literary movements should influence the development of early Indian English verse.

Thus, much of early Indian English poetry was derivative. It imitated the English models. Spontaneity and personal emotion were totally lacking. Some Indian English writers imitated their British models too closely. An interesting example is that of Ram Sharma, a prolific writer of the 1890s. He attacked an English editor of a Calcutta Daily by borrowing the very instrument that Dryden used against his enemies. Ram Sharma blatantly writes:

> Born in a garret, on low rations fed,
> Exiled from home to find in Ind his bread,
> See Skribblerus comes from beyond the main,
> With empty pockets and still emptier brain.[14]

The Romantics and the Victorians greatly influenced the Indian poets. Shelley's philosophic mind was in tune with the Indian consciousness. An early disciple of his was none other than Rabindranath Tagore. The spirit of English poetry, however, was absent. The Indian poets were too conscious of the correctness of form to give much attention to the poetic content. Linguistic excellence was achieved at the expense of significant personal emotion. The opening stanza of 'On the Banks of the Indus' is an example,

> Along the bank as here I slowly pass
> The fragrant champak with its golden hue,
> The jasmine breathing by the lemon-grass,
> The pearl datura moist with glistening dew,

Embalm the tropic air and ope to view.[15]

As is evident, the form of the poem was chiefly descriptive. Poems on Indian customs and traditions were also written in a descriptive tone. It was written primarily for an audience, and as such the over-all effect was contrived and artificial. The mark of true poetry, mainly universality, was absent.

Another kind of poetry that existed was the poetry of statement. In this type there was no attempt at suggestion. Bare ideas were stated. In fact, the writers merely took Indian philosophical ideas and conveyed it to the reader in a poetic form. Sri Aurobindo's poetry could be cited as an example. In 'Transformation' he declares:

My soul unhorizoned widens to measureless sight,
My body is God's happy living tool,
My spirit a vast sum of deathless light.[16]

There was no scope for either freshness, originality or spontaneity. The poetry of statement could be easily translated into prose. It left nothing to the imagination of the reader. The excitement of interpretation was denied. The ambivalence and complexity of later poetry was lacking. It merely became an appendix to philosophy. Philosophical ideas acquired primary importance. The poetry was only secondary. Abstraction became the general feature of this kind of poetry.

The unacknowledged birth of modern Indian English poetry occurred with the publication of Nissim Ezekiel's work in 1960. Entitled 'The Unfinished Man' it is a collection of ten poems, the most perfect so far to be written by an Indian in English. His work is a poetic record of the moral frustrations of a modern Indian in one of its own modern cities. The attention now shifted from mere description and statement to a more intriguing field, that of personal quest. Poetry was infused with significant personal emotion. Instead of being detached and objective, the writers became increasingly aware of their personal dilemmas, problems and conflicts. Poetry became for them a means of self-expression. The conflict was between the traditional and the modern. Reconciliation between the two was difficult. An Indian writing in English, for the first time, realised his rootlessness. He did not belong to the West, neither did he wholly belong to his native land. But modern Indian poetry in English acquired linguistic maturity and excellence. Poems were written on a host of themes such as family relations and ultimate philosophical questions. A few poets identified themselves with the gripping social problems that plagued urban cities.

Pritish Nandy in 'Calcutta If You Must Exile Me' cries out at the violence he finds in the streets.

> The headless corpse in the Dhakuria bylane the
> battered youth his brains blown out and the
> silent vigil that takes you to Patalaganga lane
> where they will gun you down
> without vengeance or hate.[17]

Blind acceptance of Indian culture in the 1940s gave over to critical exploration in the fifties. In the 1950s questioning was poetry. This personal quest was shared by the reader also.

The sixties was a critical decade for Indian poetry in English. The Indian poet found himself being influenced by Western sensibility, yet he could not forego his own native tradition. The two forces collided, but never merged. The quest for roots determined the poetry of the sixties. It moved inwards towards the realm of personal experience. Kamala Das spoke of her disillusionment with her husband when she bitterly wrote

> You let me sing in empty shrines,
> You let your wife
> Seek ecstasy in other's arms.[18]

The movement in the Sixties did not follow a specific course. Rather it was a movement comprising heterogeneous poets who held in their poetry different views on life and society, and on poetry itself. Yet they were linked by the common language in which they wrote.

The Seventies brought in new talent and more experimental work. English continued to hold its fascination for many young Indian writers. The result has been an increasing output of poems, some trite, some ambiguous, but occasionally some which are positively brilliant.

Deba Patnaik and Jayanta Mahapatra are two strikingly original poets from Orissa who have added a new dimension to the experimental poetry written today. R. Parthasarathy, one of our finest poets, has amply justified the individuality of the Indian English poet. His advice to young poets who look to foreign poets for material is

> Turn inward
> Scrape the bottom of your past
> Ransack the cupboard
> For skeletons
> of your Brahmin childhood. [19]

The intrinsic value of Indian English poetry is excellent by any standards. Besides reflecting the different stages of the Indian Renaissance, it has produced exquisite lyrics and narrative poems which can thrill the average reader. The Indian English poet had also evolved poetic styles of his own. There is the colloquial style of Saklatvala, the narrative style of R.C. Dutt, the simple style of Toru Dutt, the sophisticated style of Sarojini Naidu. The recent trend has been towards a compact style devoid of superfluous frills. It has resulted in a more exacting loyalty of words to ideas, image and impulse. The danger in this kind of style is that it has produced poems which are often totally deprived of romantic expression. The kind of romantic expression which Sarojini Naidu used might have ended with her. But it does not mean that romantic sensibility itself came to an end.

Only a brief survey of the birth and development of Indian English verse has been attempted here. But it is sufficient to give the general reader a concise picture of the English poetic scene in India.

References

1 Arun Shourie, *Missionaries in India: Continuities, Changes, Dilemmas* (New Delhi: ASA, 1994), p. 46.

2 *Ibid.*, pp. 65-66.

3 *Ibid.*, p. 63.

4 *Ibid.*, p. 64.

5 *Ibid.*, p. 65.

6 M.K. Naik, *A History of Indian English Literature* (New Delhi: Sahitya Akademi, 1982), p. 5.

7 *Ibid.*, p. 11.

8 R.P.N. Sinha, *The Birth and Development of Indo-English Verse*, (New Delhi: Dev, n.d), p. 35.

9 *Ibid.*, p. 48.

10 A.N. Dwivedi, *Indian Poetry in English: A Literary History and Anthology* (New Delhi: Arnold-Heinemann, 1980), p. 39.

11 *Ibid.*, p. 42.

12 *Ibid.*, p. 67.

13 *Ibid.*, p. 95.

14 V.K. Gokak, *The Golden Treasury of Indo-Anglian Poetry 1828-1965* (New Delhi: Sahitya Akademi, 1970), p. 10.

15 *Ibid.*, p. 20.

16 Dwivedi, p. 88.

17 *Indian Poetry in English*, ed. Pritish Nandy (New Delhi: Sterling, 1973), p. 40.

18 *Ibid.*, p. 36.

19 *Ibid.*, p. 22.

Chapter II

A.K. Ramanujan and Contemporary Indian Poetry in English

The last three decades have witnessed the outpouring of an immense amount of Indian English poetry which is remarkable for its polished phrasing, but which, sadly enough, lacks the essence of felt experience. The total effect has largely been literary. There was rarely an attempt to express genuine personal emotion. However, there have been a few notable exceptions. A casual assessment of the works of a few major Indian contemporary poets will prove the veracity of this statement. The basic factor involved is that they have forsaken their native language to write in a foreign tongue, English. Belonging neither here nor there, a sense of rootlessness pervaded their being, and their common quest was for a meaningful identity. This "poetry of the soul," according to M. Sivaramkrishna, "suggests one mode by which the Indian poet dissolves the basic problem he has to face as a poet: the quest for a 'usable past' whether spiritual or cultural."[1]

Seen from this angle, post-Independence Indian poetry in English, as seen in the work of Nissim Ezekiel, Kamala Das, R. Parthasarathy, A.K. Ramanujan and others may be said to have a realistic tone. The accent was on the poet's personal reaction.

The first of the post-Independence Indian poets to publish a collection of poems was Nissim Ezekiel (b. 1924). His *A Time to Change* (1952) was followed by *Sixty Poems* (1953), *The Third* (1959), *The Unfinished Man* (1960), *The Exact Name* (1965) and *Hymns in Darkness* (1976). The theme of alienation is central to his poetic work. His quest was for salvation not on a purely personal level, but on a social plane. The fairly recurrent strain in his poems is the search for belonging. In 'Background Casually,' he confesses:

> I have made my commitments now
> This is one: to stay where I am,
> As others choose to give themselves
> In some remote and backward place
> My backward place is where I am.

There is the persistent note of a sense of failure and self-doubt in his poems. Most of his poems have an urban theme. In 'City Song,' he asserts 'I don't wish to go any higher,' but:

> I want to return
> as soon as I can
> to be of the city,
> to feel its hot breath
> I have to belong.

In Ezekiel, the awareness is on the social level. The self has to be accommodated to society. He belongs to the India of hawkers and pavement sleepers, of hutment dwellers and slums, and of burnt-out mothers and frightened virgins, and wasted children and tortured animals. Though there are a number of factors in Indian life that Ezekiel dislikes, he has to adjust to its grim social reality. His struggle is a spiritual one. An important technique in Ezekiel's poem is the usage of irony. In the 'Night of the Scorpion,' the second stanza is related to the first in terms of ironic contrast. The tale is told by an observer who invests the poem with the Indian ethos and its view of evil and suffering even though he makes no claim of being a part of it. In the 'Very Indian Poem in Indian English' Ezekiel mocks the inadequate grasp of English which an average Indian has in his efforts to be termed 'cultural.' But

> I am tired
> of irony and paradox
> of the bird in the hand
> and the two in the bush
> of poetry direct and oblique
> of statement plain and symbolic. (Theological)

Ezekiel began to feel the confining influence of the sophistication in verse he had always striven for. In his later verse he moved towards a more personal and a more relaxed form of writing. In 'November Poems' he states

> Unsettle, then
> maturity of pose,
> the poise of mere experience . . .
> let existence boil
> to agonize the moralist
> within another style.

The personal theme in his poems gives rise to the autobiographical element. The most direct instance of such a poem is 'Background Casually' which concentrates mainly on the poet's background.

To Devindra Kohli, Ezekiel's failure is the failure to accept or discover or create a framework of values. His main difficulty seems to be the same as that of many other Indian poets writing in English, "Which is not as Prof. Nagarajan rather startlingly says 'they have nothing to say' but that having something valuable to say they don't seem to know where to go or how to integrate their personal discoveries into a larger and a more sustained pattern with a consistency that is the hallmark of a major poet."[2]

In contrast to Ezekiel is Kamala Das. The quest for identity is on the personal level. The focus is within. She escapes into a world of her own which leads to an upsurge of fantasy. There is no attempt to integrate the self with society as in Ezekiel. The recurring theme in her poem is the precariousness of sexual love. Her preoccupation with this could be the result of her own inherent feeling of insecurity and restlessness. Her own personality is her subject matter. Her poems are

> the speech of the mind that is
> Here and not there, a mind that sees and hears and
> Is aware. Not the deaf, blind speech
> of trees in storm or of monsoon clouds or of the rain or the

Incoherent mutterings of the blazing
Funeral pyre. (An Introduction)

Kamala Das is chiefly a poet of the modern Indian woman's ambivalence, giving expression to it more directly than any other Indian woman poet. The ambivalence in her poems arises from her dual nature, proceeding from her need for domestic security and the desire for independence from domestic restraints. When she speaks of love outside marriage she does not advocate infidelity. It is merely her search for a relationship which gives both love and security. The main drawback of her poems is that they are restricted to one personal viewpoint. This curtails her freedom to explore other themes. But such a relationship eludes her grasp, and her verse is the creative expression of her unfulfilled longings. Her initial romanticism gives way in 'The Old Playhouse' to bitter realism, for she cries:

you called me wife,
I was taught to break saccharine into your tea and
To offer at the right moment the vitamins. Cowering
Beneath your monstrous ego I ate the magic loaf and
Became a dwarf.

Her ironic conclusion is:

I am the type that endures.

Kamala Das alienated herself from critics, friends and visiting cousins who advised her not to write in English. Her alienation resulted in some of the best literature ever written in a mood of self-exploration. 'An Introduction' is a statement of her belief and her attitude to language and experience.

R. Parthasarathy is one of the few Indian poets writing in English who deliberately restrained himself from writing too many poems. His works, like Ezekiel's are conspicuous by their brilliant phrases and images. He cultivated a deliberate correctness of language and this literary finesse is evident in his poems. Parthasarathy's problem is an acute consciousness of his South Indian tradition. His poetry is concerned primarily with the question of language and identity and upon the inner conflict that arises from being brought up in two cultures. In *Rough Passage* written over a period of 15 years (1961-75), Parthasarathy deals with the theme of identity when one is exposed to two cultures. In 'Exile' he states:

> There is something to be said for exile:
> You learn roots are deep.

He returned to India from England with 'a new understanding of myself and India.' In his essay 'Whoring after English Gods' he writes: "The affair with the English language had been prolonged and tempestuous. It's over now, and I have, as the phrase goes, settled down with Tamil."[3] He even declared that he would not write poems in any other language but Tamil. Parthasarathy's dilemma was that he could not escape the tradition he had inherited. He was unable to fit its values into a meaningful framework. The feeling of being torn between two worlds resulted in his turning to Tamil. But ultimately in a mood of confessional self-disgust, he states:

> How long had it taken
> him to learn he had no talent
> at all, although words came easy.

The solution lay in reducing words to silence, and not write any poetry at all.

K.N. Daruwalla is another poet who is totally committed to the Indian scene. His poetry is concerned with the recreation of contemporary social problems. According to Ezekiel, "By depth of feeling, economy of language and originality of insight, Daruwalla commands respect."[4] His poems are a bitter criticism of contemporary social problems in India. In 'From Ruminations' and 'Routine,' he speaks of communal riots that are senseless and hate-filled.

> I can smell violence in the air
> like the lash of coming rain—
> mass hatreds drifting grey across the moon.

Scenes of violence and corruption in every sphere are the chief themes of his poems.

Other poets like Shiv K. Kumar, Jayanta Mahapatra and Arun Kolatkar deal with the personal, the social and the political in their poems.

The above poets have been discussed briefly to determine A.K. Ramanujan's position among the major parts in the post-Independence era. The conclusion that can be reached is that A.K. Ramanujan is in a class by himself. He holds a unique position in the modern Indian poetic scene. His poems like that of others is confessional. They deal with his Indian past. The search for belonging is inherent in his poems too. But the convoluted twists and turns of this search encompass a period of nearly three decades, and the conclusion arrived at is as startling as it is expected.

A.K. Ramanujan is perhaps one of the most versatile poets and translators that post-Independence India has ever known. Born in Mysore in 1929, he studied at D. Bhanumaiah's High School, and then received his B.A and M.A in English literature from the University of Mysore in 1949 and 1950 respectively. He later went to the United States of America on a Fulbright Scholarship to study folklore and linguistics at Indiana University. He received his doctorate in 1963 having already joined the faculty of the University of Chicago. He taught there for thirty years in the Department of South Asian Languages and Civilizations, and was a member of the Committee on Social Thought. During those three decades of committed academic pursuit, he inspired a whole generation of scholars in Indian literature, folklore, and linguistics, while as a poet, translator and humanist he fostered a broad understanding of Indian culture all over the world. His distinguished contribution to the field of literature brought him national and international recognition in the form of a Padmashri in 1976 from the Government of India, and a MacArthur Fellowship in 1983. In 1990, he was elected to the American Academy of Arts and Sciences. He died at the age of sixty four on 13 July 1993 while rehearsing Girish Karnad's *Naagmandala.* Ramanujan is the author of eighteen books and many influential essays. His volume of poems include *The Striders* (1966), *Relations* (1971), *Selected Poems* (1976), *Second Sight* (1986), and *The Collected Poems of A.K. Ramanujan* published posthumously in 1995. The last volume includes a collection of poems entitled *The Black Hen*. The earliest of the poems in this volume appear to have been written in 1989, in Michigan, and the latest in March or April 1993. The poems in the earlier volumes have, as S. Nagarajan puts it, "their origin in recollected personal emotion. They deal with the poet's memory of his relations and the ambiguous freedom that life away from them confers."[5] Ramanujan moved to Chicago with concrete memories of his life in India. His theme is announced in the epigraph poem, a translation from Tamil,

> Like a hunted deer
> On the wide white
> Salt land,
>   A flayed hide
>   turned inside out,
> One may run,
> escape.
>   But living
> among relations
> binds the feet.[6] (56)

A.K. Ramanujan is a poet whose creative tension arises from a powerful memory sharpened by physical distance. Though settled in America, the central motifs of his poems evolve from a recollection of the memories associated with his Indian past. The memories are not merely recollected to sentimentalize over, but are ingeniously used to exorcise memory itself. The process is excruciating, for the persona speaks in a language that repeatedly reflects a recurrent quest for a sense of rootedness. Caught between the opposing forces of Westernization and his own native tradition, Ramanujan's poetry shows psychologically creative tension. Realism mingled with the problems of a bi-cultural and bi-lingual situation forms the basis of his self-analysis.

In poetry this conflict is dramatised, and an attempt is made to resolve the psychic tension. From early times, man has attempted to crystallize 'reality' in figurative speech. Words, as Cleanth Brooks says, open out into the larger symbolizations on all levels—for example, into archetypal symbol, ritual, and myth. The archetypal patterns in poetry provide a clue as to how its formal structure is related to the basic patterns in our psyche. The Indian theory of *samskara* finds a parallel here. The emotional significance of certain poems is the result of the "primordial images" or archetypes which are aroused in the mind of the reader on reading them. Jung describes these archetypes as the "psychic residue of numberless experiences of the same type."

Ramanujan's poetry opens out the possibilities of realizing these primordial images in the form of literary symbols. The poet re-creates long forgotten memories, and the reader re-lives it aesthetically. These images are evocative, and the persona's dilemma is thus expressed in imagistic verse. There is no attempt to contemporize the past as in Parthasarathy's poems. Parthasarathy sought to neutralize the past with images from the present, and these images are contextual. But Ramanujan could neither escape from the past nor could he effectively co-relate it with the present. As such, in his poems there is no pervasive conflict between self and society as in the poetry of Nissim Ezekiel.

The content of Ramanujan's poetry is extremely Indian. The main experience in his poetry is connected with his family and his horde of relations. Yet, though his poems were intensely personal, he sought to universalize his personal predicament. In 'Love Poem for a Wife,' he transcends purely personal emotion and tries to universalize the concept of Hindu marriage. In this poem Ramanujan moves from one idea to another with no logical sequence. In the last two stanzas, he seeks to provide a solution to rectify drifting marriages in the Indian context. The remedy is to either marry your sister as the Egyptians did 'to continue the incests/of childhood into marriage,' or 'as well meaning/hindus did' betroth them before birth so that marriage could be carried back into 'the namelessness of childhood.' (67) The poem is an ironic analysis of his own marriage. The very title of the poem is ironic. In the process, he mocks the Indian way of life. Though the poem has its roots in his personal predicament, it has a universal significance in that it talks about the universal problem of a drifting marriage.

In 'Still Another View of Grace' the conflict of two cultures, Western and Indian, is dramatically juxtaposed. The two sets of values are equally attractive, but the poet's dilemma lies in making the choice. The Eastern concept of chastity is placed against the Western concept of free love. The poet's physical distance from his native land reinforces his personal dilemma. The conflict between the two sets of values is inherent in the poem. Though a citizen of America, he does not accept its culture. He still clings to the tradition he has inherited. In the poem, 'thought' is personified as a woman of easy virtue. The 'thought' is the thought of illicit love. The freedom to love the poet finds in the West is heady in its intoxication. In the beginning, his Indian conservatism holds him back, for he turns back and catches hold of

> that thought
> by the screams of her hair and said: 'Beware.
> Do not follow a gentleman's morals
> with that absurd determined air.
> Find a priest. Find any beast in the wind
> for a husband.' (45)

The intention here is to legalize the consummation of desire through marriage. But he succumbs to the allure of this forbidden thought, and

> commandments crumbled
> in my father's past. Her tumbled hair suddenly known
> as silk in my angry hand, I shook a little and
> took her, behind the laws of my land (45)

In this poem abstract notions of morality are concretized in a personal predicament, and this lends an authenticity to Ramanujan's work. The poem ironically repudiates all the values that the Brahmins stand for. The poem has a distinct confessional note.

On the other hand, it satirizes the complacent spiritual attitude of the Indians.

In 'History,' Ramanujan reminiscences about the avaricious and callous nature of a particular pair of aunts. The day his great aunt died, her two daughters, one dark and one fair, unknown to each other, alternatively divested their mother's body before it was cold

> of diamond ear-rings,
> bangles, anklets, the pin
> in her hair,
> the toe-rings from her wedding
> the previous century,
> all except the gold
> in her teeth and the silver g-string
> they didn't know she wore
> her napkins on. (108)

The ornaments described are those that would belong to a typical South Indian orthodox Brahmin woman. The poem is, again, ironical in content. The usually expressionless face of his dark aunt acquired some 'expression at last' when she realised her perfidy was known to all. The poem also mocks the fact that even in their last hours, the dead are not left alone. A death in an Indian family was a momentous event:

> With all those children in and out
> of the death-room, all the kith and kin
> milling in the kitchen, wet faggot smoke
> and rumours about the will (108)

Scant respect was paid to the dead. Morbid curiosity drew all the kith and kin rather than genuine sorrow.

As in other Indian poets, the theme of disharmony is also found in Ramanujan's poems. In 'Take Care,' however, the suggestion of violence is placed in a Western context.

> In Chicago,
> do not walk slow.
> Find no time

> to stand and stare,
> Down there, blacks look black
> And whites, they look blacker. (104)

The superficiality of women in general, and their inability or reluctance to think deeply is attacked by Ramanujan in the poem 'Any Cow's Horn Can Do It.' He says:

> Any number of things
> Can make a woman like awake

And then he continues:

> But nothing you say with words
> In a poem will make her scream
> get sick, or go grey in the face.

His ironic conclusion is:

> Poems aren't even words
> Enough to rankle, infect
> Or make the smallest incisions
> Unless wife, girl friend or sister . . .
> somehow are
> made to think it's all about
> their shame in the market, or
> an elegy on the death
> of a far-off cousin. (94)

The poet's disillusionment with poems providing the means for understanding and harmony is evident here.

The cheapness of life is narrated brilliantly in 'A Minor Sacrifice.' But in a world of senseless killing, there also appears to be the possibility of poetic justice as in the strange 'grass-hopper like' death of Shivanna. In the volume of poems entitled 'Second Sight,' there is the juxtaposition of tradition with modernity. Poems like 'Elements of Composition,' 'Ecology,' 'No Amnesiac King' and 'In the Zoo' among others reiterate the harsh and brittle quality of modern existence. Cynicism coupled with disillusionment, related to the traditional and the modern, form the basic tenor of the poems in this volume.

The persona in Ramanujan's poems is very thinly disguised. The background of his poems was highly traditional in most cases. It chiefly belonged to the orthodox setting of his Brahmin ancestry in South India. His personal tragedy was that he was an expatriate. He could not identify himself wholly with the West or with the East. In his search for identity, he drifted alone as the title of his first volume *The Striders* suggests. His quest was to find basic meaningful relations. Personal relations are not the result of rational choice, but the result of heredity and tradition. From this dilemma, his entire poetry emerges.

References

1 M. Sivaramkrishna, "Contemporary Indian Poetry in English: An Approach," *Opinion Literary Quarterly*, Vol. I, Monsoon Issue, (No publishing detail), p. 52

2 Devindra Kohli, "Indian Poetry in English: Two Views," *The Journal of Commonwealth Literature*, Vol. IX, No. 1, ed. Arthur Ravenscroft (Oxford Univ. Press, 1974), p. 24.

3 "Whoring after English Gods," *Perspectives*, ed. S.P. Bhagwat (Bombay: Popular, 1970), pp. 43-60.

4 *Contemporary Indian Poetry in English*, ed. Saleem Peeradina (Bombay: Macmillan, 1972), p. 67.

5 *Ibid.*, p. 18.

6 *The Collected Poems of A.K. Ramanujan* (Delhi: Oxford University Press, 1995), p. 56. All further references to this text are indicated by page numbers in parenthesis.

Chapter III

Thematic and Imagistic Pattern in A.K. Ramanujan's Poetry

To read any of Ramanujan's poems is to be charmed by his wit and ingenuity and a language which owes its superb energy to an 'enacting eye.'[1] The poems in his volumes have not been arranged in a chronological order. To the uninitiated reader, the poems ostensibly bear no relation to each other. Like the coloured pieces of glass in a kaleidoscope, his poems appear isolated and attractive. But a practised shake can make the coloured pieces merge into a delightful pattern. It is the same with Ramanujan's poems. A discerning reader will be pleasantly surprised at the secrets which the poems yield. They provide an amazing clue to an understanding of the poet's personality. The apparently unconnected poems now take on a definite pattern, each bearing a definite relation to the other. By this ingenious method, Ramanujan easily ensures the sustained interest of his readers. It goes to his credit that he can achieve this difficult task with effortless ease.

Images play a decisive role in Ramanujan's poetry. It is through them that he communicates his ideas. An image in his poem is used graphically to elaborate a particular thought. The skilled use of metaphors is another proof of Ramanujan's superb craftsmanship. As a poet he realised he could find a release for his agonising mental conflicts only by giving them expression in imagistic verse. An understanding of the imagery employed by him is thus highly essential to the understanding of Ramanujan as a poet. The images are the links which give a total picture of the poet's personality.

Since the poems have not been arranged methodically, it is necessary to find a key poem to which the other poems can be related. 'Self-Portrait' is the poem in this instance which provides the central theme. This poem provides an insight into the reality behind the mask which the persona of the poems wear. Torn by opposing values, the poet reveals his helpless position in 'Self-Portrait.'

> I resemble everyone
> but myself.[2] (23)

The protagonist in the poem is one who has lost his identity. The poetry of Ramanujan reveals its authentic sense of modernity. Modern man has lost his roots. He has no anchorage, his life is characterised by aimless drifting. The loss of roots is reflected in the distorted image in the mirror. The mirror instead of reflecting the poet's image, 'despite the well-known laws/of optics' reflects the portrait of a stranger. The mirror is distorted because it does not reflect reality. The poet's quest for identity is in vain. Periodically, the mirror reflects the image of his father. The portrait of the stranger is signed in the corner by his father. Part of the poet's identity is thus preserved by his father. The father represents stable values, values with which the son has disassociated himself. The loss of values in the son is metaphorically represented by loss of image in the mirror. But try as he might the son cannot entirely detach himself from his inherited tradition. The signature of his father is his reminder that these values cannot be easily and entirely forsaken. The father is then the poet's connection with his inherited culture. The irony is that though his search for identity is futile, yet a part of his identity is preserved in his father. 'Self-Portrait' thus becomes the main theme in Ramanujan's quest for identity. Since the father is the central figure in the poem, by implication, the themes of his poems are bound to be familial in context.

If this metaphor of the mirror is extended, then the other poems are facets which reflect parts of the poet's personality. The irony is that the total reflected image does not portray the image of the poet. His search does not end, but continues hopelessly.

His image is distorted into the picture of his father. The conclusion that can be arrived at is that from the past, his father, though long since dead, continues to grip his sensibility. The poet's personality is completely dwarfed under the overwhelming influence of his father's personality.

Since the father is a dominating influence in the poet's life, it is necessary to examine the overall background of the father in an effort to examine the inherited culture of the son. The tension in Ramanujan's poetry arises from the conflict between his inherited and acquired values.

'A River' is the best poem to be dealt with in regard to this aspect. The river which flows through the city of Madurai is a symbol of timelessness. It represents the eternal flow of culture, the culture of his father. Madurai, earlier, was the city of temples, symbolising the spiritual culture of man. His father belonged to this highly spiritual, conservative and traditional background. It is this culture which has been inherited by the son. To the poets who sang of cities and temples, spiritual attainment was considered the highest mark of civilisation. Madurai was the city of the religious nature of the Indian ethos. The temple is a graphic image for it represents a paradigm of Indian culture. But now,

> every summer
> a river dries to a trickle
> in the sand,
> baring the sand-ribs,
> straw and women's hair
> clogging the watergates
> at the rusty bars
> under the bridges with patches
> of repair all over them,
> the wet stones glistening like sleepy
> crocodiles, the dry ones
> shaven water-buffaloes lounging in the sun. (38)

The drying of the river metaphorically suggests the present sterility of the poet's culture. Modernisation results in disintegration. The once stable values now give way under the onslaught of Westernization. The very imagery in the poem reveals the stagnation of the poet's culture. The wet stones are immobile, like sleepy crocodiles, the dry stones are as still as shaven water-buffaloes lounging in the sun. The evident disintegration of the culture cannot be stopped. The bars are rusty, and the bridge has patches of repair all over it. The father's values which the son has inherited crumble under the force of his acquired Western values.

The poets now ironically sang only of the floods. They were fascinated by the Western values which gradually corroded the foundation of their culture. They sang of the pregnant woman and the couple of cows which the floods carried away. Symbolically it suggests the affluence and prosperity of traditional India which were swept away by the rising tide of modernisation. In its wake, modernisation did not leave anything worthwhile and stable, but only bared sand-ribs. Our attempts at modernity are futile. Madurai was formerly a city of culture, where the poets drew their inspiration from its spiritual heritage. But now, under the recurring impact of modern sensibility, the slow process of disintegration begins.

Disintegration involves the break up of a culture, resulting in instability. It is out of this struggle between two sets of values that the poet's sensibility arises. He can neither give up the past, nor can he reconcile himself to the present. In the process, he loses his identity. The poet as such, is in no way entitled to judge his culture since he does not entirely belong to it. The poem gives a general picture of a total culture.

Now that the poet's inherited culture has been analysed, the next step is to focus on the poet's personality which has been moulded by this inherited tradition. In 'Case-History,' there is a vivid analysis of the poet's predicament. The very title of the poem suggests the poet to be a psychic case. The term is commonly used in psychology to indicate a truncated consciousness. The poet finds this term applicable in his own case. His mental retardation is the result of his cloistered and stiflingly conservative and traditional background. In the poem, the poet wonders in retrospect, and seeks to find the reason for his personal tragedy.

> What had he done
> to crush glass in his fist
> one middle-aged morning, known
> only as morning by clocks without the sun? (47)

The opening line echoes a typical Indian sentiment in that every present misfortune is related to an ignoble deed in the past. The image of the 'crushed glass' is related to the mirror of 'Self-Portrait.' Glass is a recurring image in Ramanujan's poems. Crushed glass indicates the loss of identity which must have been a painful realisation. Though he was middle-aged, the poet had not yet realised his true self. Darkness still enveloped his sensibilities. The poet does not understand why he should accept Western values unquestioningly. His retarded mentality does not allow him to recognize the identity he might have possessed in the past. In an effort to re-discover himself, he attempts to probe into his past. But

> At seven, his slingshot had not hit
> the frosted childhood's streetlight. (47)

The imagery employed is extremely subtle. The poet's childhood is compared to a streetlight. Though a streetlight is common property, it sheds its light on a limited area. As a child, the poet's sensibilities were denied a healthy development. Bound by conventions, he grew up with a retarded consciousness. His reason was not allowed to develop. 'Slingshot' is an effective metaphor symbolising the poet's reason. His mental development did not synchronise with his physical growth. His childhood was thus frosted, his sensibilities dimmed, and now, even as an adult, he was unable to transcend the innocence of his childhood, for

> he was no looting horseback Hun
> out of his history books. (47)

The instrument of reason had not dispelled the misty errors of his childhood. He was an undeveloped, immature traditional child, and he remained thus even in his later years. The poet was no 'looting horseback Hun.' He was depressingly docile. He accepted his tradition uncomplainingly. He did not have the courage to oppose traditional values, and neither did he have the initiative to examine his inherited tradition. The result was a frosted consciousness. The poet has not metaphorically exposed himself to reason, and neither has he metaphorically crossed the threshold of innocence.

> on
> evenings full of bat's wings
> he had scarcely seen a sister raped by
>   a dead father's sin
> but only shaped by a mother's word (47)

Most Indians are like bats. The image is simple but devastating in its effect. The bats see only in the dark—only darkness exists for them. There is no room for light, since light is not recognised by them. Indians still cling to their ancient tradition. Most of them refuse to leave this darkness. Averse to knowledge which could dispel superstition and false values, they have not yet acquired the rationality to examine their own unexamined tradition. Naturally they are like bats content with the darkness which enfolds them. The poet himself is like one of these bats. His sister was no help either. As he was docile, she was servile. Both were shackled by the iron grip of tradition.

> In
> the swirl of his teens he had perhaps thrilled
> to raisin thefts and one kiss under the stairs. Once he ran
> from a body house without windows
> looking for the wombs of faceless women
> he never filled
> with sons. (47)

In his teens the poet did things, carried away by unstable emotions. He never had the courage to follow his convictions. The height of daring was to steal a kiss under the stairs, or indulge in petty thefts. Being emotionally inhibited, he grew up without acquiring the stature of a man. Frustrated, he attempted to seek emotional satisfaction. But his inhibitions were so constricting that he never filled the wombs of faceless women with sons. He compares his body to a house without windows, without channels for expression. His yearnings remained unfulfilled, his hopes remained unrealised.

He could not transcend his mental blocks. His emotional life was thus starved, and this led to his stunted growth, and his imbalanced personality. As a child he was 'frosted,' as an adolescent he was starved, and

> now he has glass in his fist
> and several rows
> of futures that could not reach any past. (47)

Now he is a faceless person, a person without an identity, sterile and in a vacuum, unable to connect the past with the future. Too late has he acquired the knowledge which could have helped him in the past.

'Case-History' is a brilliant poem where the poet vividly dramatises the problem of a split personality, of a truncated consciousness. His tragedy was that he was not courageous enough to free himself from his inhibited milieu. The poet establishes himself as a psychic case.

This, then is the poet's background. This, then is the cause of his present tragedy. But there were various other factors responsible for his truncated consciousness. The father is an important figure in contemporary literature. More often than not, he is presented as a symbol of meaningless tyranny. The father is a recurring image in his poems. 'Case-History' takes us to the father-figure in 'Obituary.' "Father, when he passed on," the poet observes:

> left dust
> on a table full of papers,
> left debts and daughters. (111)

The son ironically criticizes his father. His father did not command respect or admiration. He never left behind anything that could inspire his son. Never having been a source of inspiration in his life, he was less so in death. Instead of leaving behind a spiritual or cultural legacy, the father bequeathed his son with the unfinished, muddled business of his life. He left dust on a table full of papers, debts, and daughters, which were another form of responsibility. The father's life had been chaotic, and in death also the chaos did not end with him. Rather it survived him, thus symbolising the manner in which the father had mismanaged his life. The father was a failure, and the son who was highly influenced by him, remained maladjusted and a psychic. Even two generations later, the poet's son caustically referred to as 'a bed-wetting grandson' was a replica of the poet's father. The whole race was gradually degenerating. The father also left behind

> a house that leaned
> slowly through our growing
> years on a bent coconut
> true in the yard. (111)

The leaning house metaphorically means the deterioration of traditional values. The physical description is evocative here of a general condition of decay. The normal procedure when a house needs repair would be to repair it. But in this instance, the poet is indifferent to the steadily deteriorating house. This indicated the poet's disassociation with his culture. The culture which could have provided him with a sound foundation is thus discarded. The poet's restlessness arises from this. As the poet grew in years, so did his disassociation with his culture. The leaning house is paradoxically juxtaposed with the bent coconut tree. Deterioration is evident everywhere. The growing consciousness of the poet ironically coincides with the collapse of the house. It is an ironic double process. In the poem there is a juxtaposition of tradition and modernity. This is indicated by the images in the following extract. After the cremation, the ashes of the father are taken by the sons to

> throw as the priest
> said, facing east

where three rivers met
near the railway station. (111)

Ramanujan uses a crucial traditional image. 'As the priest said' indicates a typical Indian belief in tradition and superstition. The sons are not intellectually liberated. They blindly followed the customs of their ancestors. The river is again a traditional symbol indicating not only the ancient culture in India, but also the relentless passage of time. But the railway station where the three rivers met is a jarring symbol of modernity, the result of Westernization. In Ramanujan's poem, there is a constant mixture of tradition and modernity.

The father's death was indifferently greeted by his sons. It was as if he had never existed. Once the ashes were swallowed by the river, there was no evidence of the father's existence. There was

no longstanding headstone
with his full name and two dates
to hold in their parenthesis
everything he didn't quite
manage to do himself. (111)

The father had been a non-entity in life, so was he in death. In his life-time, he had been a hopeless failure. He did nothing noble for which he could have perhaps been remembered with honour and love. His insignificant life came to a close with his death.

The father's birth was unnatural, as the phrase 'Caesarian birth' underlines. He was born in a Brahmin Ghetto, isolated from the ordinary movement of life. He died in isolation too—not in the midst of his family, but alone in the fruit market of heart failure. Born unnaturally, he lived unnaturally, and died unnaturally too. The poet ironically juxtaposes death, a symbol of decay, with fruits, the symbol of regeneration. The father was a product of technical triumph (caesarian) but a victim of twentieth century bustle, which induces heart failure.

The father's death makes no impact on the son. Totally indifferent to the whole episode, he hears of the obituary from someone who told him

he got two lines
in an inside column
of a Madras newspaper

which was ironically

sold by the kilo
exactly four weeks later
to street hawkers (111)

who sold it in turn to the small groceries where the poet bought jaggery, salt and coriander in newspaper cones that he usually read for fun. This time he bought it in the hope of finding the obituary lines. The mention of places in Ramanujan's poetry is symbolic of its culture. Madras symbolises the citadel of South Indian culture. The father, ironically, a non-entity in life, gets an insignificant mention in a significant paper. The father's death is connected with the living presence of the son for the paper comes back to him in the form of a newspaper cone.

The father besides leaving them with poverty, also left them with

a changed mother
    and more than
one annual ritual. (111)

The poet is left with his mother, so it's only appropriate that the figure of the mother should now be analysed. The mother is another recurring image in Ramanujan's poetry. Together with the father, the mother also influenced the poet's life to a great extent.

In 'Of mothers, among other things,' he painfully reminiscences about his mother.

I smell upon this twisted
Blackbone tree the silk and white
petal of my mother's youth. (61)

Colour symbolism is an integral part of the poem. The twisted blackbone tree could indicate the bent and aged black body of his mother. Visualising this pathetic figure, the poet is also able to conjure a vision of her beautiful youth. He refers to it as 'the silk and white petal,' which is an extremely expressive metaphor.

> From her ear-rings three diamonds
> splash a handful of needles
> and I see my mother run back
> from rain to the crying cradles. (61)

The needles symbolise the eternal questioning of the mother's life which is inarticulate. The three diamonds in her ear are a symbol of domesticity. But instead of splashing a handful of light, they splash a handful of needles. Being a mother has brought her innumerable sufferings. Her suffering is silent, her sorrows remain unexpressed. She cannot break loose from the chains which bind her because of the 'crying cradles.' Her children are the binding ties from which she can never cut herself off. The cradle thus becomes a symbol of stability and responsibility.

> Like the rains which
> . . . tack and sew
> with broken thread the rags
> of the tree-tasselled light (61)

The poet gets flashes of memory, which recreates the past. In these flashes, he sees his mother,

> But her hands are a wet eagle's
> two black pink-crinkled feet,
> one talon crippled in a garden—
> trap set for a mouse. (61)

The mother's drenched hands symbolise the torrential experiences which continuously drain her of all energy. Her hands are compared to the feet of an eagle. Ramanujan evokes a mood through mere physical description. This is the 'enacting eye' for which he has been justly praised. The eagle is a symbol of soaring flight, of soaring ambitions, of soaring desires. The mother, before domesticity enslaved her, perhaps had had these longings too. But now one talon is crippled in a garden trap set for a mouse. The mother is trapped by her obligations to her family like a mouse caught in a trap. In this iron mesh of domesticity, the mother pays a heavy price, she loses her individuality. She becomes a timid, docile being like the mouse. There is no way of escape from the cage she has built around her. The mother's soaring ambitions are now crippled.

> Her sarees
> do not cling: they hang, loose
> feather of a one time wing (61)

Her youth had been spent in this repressed atmosphere. Now in her old age, she grows more and more self-effacing, until not a spark of her former spirit remains. Her 'one time wing' has now been fully and effectively clipped.

> My cold parchment tongue licks bark
> in the mouth when I see her four
> still sensible fingers slowly flex
> to pick a grain of rice from the kitchen floor (61)

The poet watches his mother's plight helplessly. He can only observe and grieve at this predicament. He is powerless to help her escape. She grows old and ineffective, still bound by tradition, and the memory of her now only brings him a sharp sense of agony. His creativity as a poet becomes sterile in the universal suffering of mothers. In this poem, Ramanujan gives a tragic picture of the slow dwindling of a personality in the presence of convention and tradition. His mother was a victim to it. So was he. His present state of bewilderment and helplessness can be linked up with this background of his mother.

The poet's mother and father were important in shaping the poet's sensibility. It has now been clearly established that his father was a failure and his mother a symbol of domestic sterility. The poet himself had no domestic felicity. Marriage does not bring him the emotional happiness he had dreamt of . The same pattern of failure recurred in his domestic life too. 'Love Poem for a Wife. I' speaks of his incompatible marriage. Married to a Keralite who gave no proof of her love for him, the marriage was a predestined failure. The reason the poet gives for their emotional separation is 'unshared childhood.' The emotion they share is not of immediacy, but a nostalgia for the past.

In the transverse midnight gossip
of cousins reunions among
brandy fumes, cashews and the absences
of grand parents, you suddenly grow
nostalgic for my past and I
envy you your village dog-ride
and the mythology
of the seven crazy aunts. (65)

The wife is as nostalgic about her husband's past as he is of hers. But reconciliation is impossible for the emotional barriers they have created can never be destroyed. The wife recognises her husband only 'In the albums/of family rumour, in brothers/ anecdotes of how noisily/father bathed,/slapping soap on his back.' In India, the son's identity is merely an extension of his father's. The father is an alter-ego of the son. Through this poem, Ramanujan seeks to establish his identity. The poet's father was servile, and demanded obedience from his son. The poet says the father sought to

reduce the entire career
of my recent unique self
to the compulsion of some high
sentence in his Smilesian diary. (66)

The father had gained knowledge about enforcing discipline from the works of Smiles, and he attempted to put them into practice on his son. The result: the son too turned servile like the father.

The wife's father was no better. Her father was now senile, 'gone irrevocable in age.' Her youth had been reduced by him to one of frightening suppression, for

He will acknowledge the wickedness
of no reminiscence: not, not
the burning end of the cigarette
in the balcony, pacing
to and fro as you come to the gate,
late, after what you thought
was an innocent
date with a nice Muslim friend
who only hinted at touches. (66)

The relation between the father and daughter was abnormal. There was no understanding or trust between them. The father refused to remember his daughter's teenage days because he did not want to acknowledge his lack of control over her. The 'burning end of the cigarette' symbolises the flickering end of his own control over her. The father was tyrannical, and so the daughter had to find an outlet for her normal desires in surreptitious experiences, like a date with a 'nice' Muslim friend who hinted only at touches. The wife, like the poet, thus grew up emotionally inhibited. She, too, was the product of an unnatural psyche. Between two people coming from such an abnormal background, emotional rapport was all the more difficult.

The relationship between them was sterile. The wife could only talk of trivialities with her brother. The poet bitterly comments:

you wagered heirlooms
    and husband's earnings on what
the Uncle in Kuwait
would say about the Bathroom
and the well. (67)

The existing relationship between them was thus commercialized. The wife had no qualms about wagering her husband's earnings on meaningless bets. Money is here used to convey the absence of the basic emotion of love.

The mention of various places in the poem like the poet's present residence in Chicago, his wife's father's house in Aleppey, her uncle in Kuwait is deviously used by the poet to symbolise modern rootlessness. The family is the unit of Indian culture. The disruption of the family indicates the break-up of this culture. The poet and his wife belonged to a culture that was deteriorating steadily.

In 'Love Poem for Wife. 2,' the poet continues to elaborate on the incompatibility between himself and his wife. The poem begins on a note of dissonance,

> After a night of rage,
> that lasted days,
> quarrels in a forest. (83)

and then the poet moves on to speak about his 'wife's always/ changing syriac face,' 'a pouting difficult child's/changing in the chameleon, emerald/wilderness of Kerala.' The poet realises too late that he had chosen a moody and unstable woman for a wife. She was 'small cousin' to the tall mythic men of Kerala. The image of 'small cousin' suggests a woman of puny nature, in direct contrast to the mythical men of heroic stature who belonged to Kerala, her native land. The wife was a symbol of sterile sensibility.

The poet then switches on to her grandmother who had spent her childhood in a village in Kerala 'full of the colour schemes/ of kraits and garter snakes,' her adolescence was spent 'in Aden among stabbing/Arabs' in a land of 'borrowed earth/under the borrowed streets.' Physically and culturally his wife's background was uprooted as his.

> I dreamed one day
> that face my own yet hers,
> with my own nowhere
> to be found; lost; cut
> loose like my dragnet
> past. (84)

There is an ironic reference to the poem 'Self-Portrait.' The poet feels a peculiar identity with his wife's grandmother. The wife's face resembles the grandmother's—logically then the poet should have realised his identity in his wife. But the ironic paradox is that though legally his wife belongs to him, yet in her face he does not find his image. Once again his search for identity is futile. On waking up, he discovers the harsh reality in

> half a mirror
> in the mountain cabin
> fallen behind the dresser. (84)

A full mirror symbolises the union of husband and wife as a composite entity. But the poet recognises only half an image of himself in the mirror. The other half is lost forever in his wife. According to Indian philosophy, a man remained incomplete until and unless he acquired complete knowledge of his wife. Lord Shiva is represented as half-man and half-woman. But the poet is only half a man. The husband and wife thus have separate identities. There is no possibility of their ever merging into a harmonious whole.

The poet is happy only in his dream. On waking up, he discovers he is

> soon to be myself, a man
> unhappy in the morning
> to be himself again,
> the past still there,
> a drying
> net on the mountain. (85)

With daylight, reason returns. Metaphorically, he cannot endure the pitiless light for he has lost his face. Unhappy memories of a sterile past which is evoked by the image of a drying net on a mountain, return, and he is compelled to return reluctantly to his sterile present. The poet is envious of his wife who is

> still fast
> asleep, blessed as by
> butterfly, snake, shiprope,
> and grandmother's other
> children,
> by my only love's only
> insatiable envy. (85)

Unlike the first love poem, the wife is here metaphorically able to sleep. She is unassailed by the psychic disturbances which plague her husband. Contentedly she lives in a cocoon utterly alienated from her husband. The husband envies her this peace which constantly eludes him. In the first poem, the problem of unshared childhood is at least shared by them. But now the husband suffers alone. The movement in the poem is from the present to the past, and then back to the present again.

Yet, even in his misery, hope still lingers in his breast. In the poem 'It Does Not Follow, But When in the Street,' he sees

> yellow trees bend over broken glass
> and the walls of Central Jail
> drip with spring's laburnum
> yellows, yellow on yellow. (57)

The broken glass symbolises the psychic disturbances which seek to expunge his personality. Central Jail is a symbol of hopelessness. But yellow trees bend over broken glass, and the walls of Central Jail are profusely covered with the flowers of spring, which are a symbol of life and hope. Ramanujan uses the clever technique of juxtaposition. The symbol of destruction, such as broken glass, is cancelled by the yellow trees, which are symbolic of hope. Looking at the creativity around him, the poet forgets the eczema on his feet and the holes in his shoe. He dreams of the bright and secure future he might have the happiness to enjoy. The images of sterility are thus cancelled by the images of creativity. Nature lifts him from the despondency he has sunk into. It generates hope, and he says:

> I walk on air
> I walk on water, can even bear
> to walk on earth for my wife
> and I will someday somehow share
> a language, a fire, a clean first floor
> with a hill in the window; and eat
> on an ancient sandalwood door. (57)

He dreams of the day when he will be able to communicate with his wife in the language of shared emotions. To achieve this, he was prepared to suffer any amount of misery. He dreams of comfort and 'a clean first floor.' This phrase has a Freudian interpretation. According to Freud, the human mind has two floors. The first floor contains all the suppressed desires, and the second floor contains the thoughts that are ordinarily communicated. In fact, it means the façade or the mask a person puts on. Only when the suppressed desires and inhibitions are released, can the person hope to achieve a healthy personality. The poet optimistically hopes that the shared language with his wife will cleanse his first floor. He hopes it will purify him so that they can begin their life on an auspicious note, as is suggested by the image of eating 'on an ancient sandalwood door.'

The central theme in this poem does not follow from one image. Images are juxtaposed in such a manner that they suggest a psychic rebirth. All this does not follow from logic, but in the street when he sees the symbols of sterility jostling against the symbols of creativity, his leaden heart lightens, and his optimism soars. From this juxtaposition, the poet arrives at a personal equation. He comes to terms with himself. And it is Nature which regenerates his hope.

The poet's background has so far been examined from the microcosm of the family. Let us now examine the macrocosm of the social and cultural milieu to which Ramanujan belongs. Taken in the wider context of tradition and culture, the poem 'One Reads' gives an insight into this aspect of the poet's background. Daily, and therefore calmly, one reads:

> of the raving Ganges,
> the boats overturned;
> a summer's thatch of villages
> most casually burned. (48)

The very opening of the poem is ironic. One reads and is calm, because reading of such events has become monotonous in its regularity. There is no incentive to participate. The average Indian does not experience the reality of authentic India. The tragedy of the persona is that his cultivated indifference does not allow him to participate in the problems of his country. 'The raving Ganges' and 'the boats overturned' are symbolic of destruction by nature. Nature is unpredictable, and so her actions can be pardoned, but man has rejoiced in his art of inflicting torture. The wanton destruction of the villages suggested by the image of the villages being casually burned is ample evidence. Then again, one reads about

> our night's pomegranate mines
> that cast
> their amber seeds
> into the future and the changing past
> of files, charts and last year's twins,
> the once-tended hives
> in the garden
> or even
> the unwaiting sociable wives. (48)

India, the garden, has run to seed. In her efforts to industrialize herself, the present has been forgotten in favour of the past and the future. We read about the pomegranate mines, symbolising the numerous efforts at modernity, which will cast their amber seeds, symbolising the benefits of such modernity, into the distant future. Or we read about the past symbolised by the files and charts which suggest the bureaucratic delay prevalent in Government offices. The present, which matters, is forgotten. The once-tended hives crumble and decay. The ancient heritage of India which was glorious once, is now forgotten, and the result is the meaningless and mechanical age. Ramanujan juxtaposes inanimate images like files and charts with animate images like twins and wives to get an ironic incongruity.

> But through the tall headlines
> one hears now and then
> the ambushed silence (48)

The 'tall headlines' suggest the tall claims made by the Indians about their rationality. But ironically, this rationality is smothered. They have not acquired the intellectual courage to examine the tradition, which continues to grip their sensibilities. The lone voice of protest against the existing condition is immediately 'ambushed.' One also reads about

the pebbled ebb of crested tides
where no one rides
upright:
the wildcat quiet
of evil in distant worlds,
the narrowing spiral of reeling birds
and bankrupt brood that hatch like lice
in other men's Sunday suns. (48)

A graphic image of twentieth century India is evoked by the images present in this extract. 'Crested tides' suggest the false claims of Indians to all the virtuous qualities. The dismal reality is that none of them have the courage of their convictions. Hence, in this tide no one rides upright. Another aspect of Indian hypocrisy is evoked by the image of 'the wildcat quiet of evil in distant worlds.' Indians have tasted the fruits of Western culture. Like wildcats they have tasted blood and still hunger for more. But when confronted with it, they pretend ignorance. The next image of 'the reeling birds,' and the bankrupt brood that hatch like lice give a sordid aspect of Indian life. No rationality governs their actions. They breed like lice, smug in the knowledge that if their own Government cannot support them, it will have no other alternative but to beg for foreign aid. Then, one sees

the leprosy of light and shade,
the sunlit beggar squatting
on his shadow, clotting
the antlers of bare April's trees:
pandering lies
for our charity's
counterfeit pice. (49)

When all these aspects of Indian society are considered, the future seems depressing indeed. Indian mentality is leprous, a mingling of light and shade, of knowledge and ignorance. In this poem, reading, hearing and visualising are juxtaposed to give an ironic picture of a degenerate and decaying society.

The probable reason for this calm indifference is suggested in the poem 'The Hindoo' he reads his *Gita* and is calm at all events. The Indian calmness towards all events is the result of Indian philosophy. Indian philosophy, which began on an idealistic note, is now degraded. The sacred text of the *Gita* preached the concept of non-attachment. The idea was to preserve a balance, a poise in life. But,

> At this party heads have no noses, teeth close
> upon my heart: yet I come unstuck
> and stand apart. I do not marvel
> when I see good and evil. (79)

'Heads' symbolise intellect. But in this activity, heads have no noses, or the capacity for feeling. Even the sharp bite of some memory does not evoke any emotion. The poet deliberately stifles it. He comes unstuck and stands apart. He does not allow any emotion to involve him deeply. Good and evil have become relative. He has reached the supreme stage of indifference where neither good nor evil has the ability to excite or depress him. This philosophy, the poet ironically suggests, is derived from the Hindu tradition which professes the maintenance of a state of neutrality at all events to be the highest virtue.

> I just walk
> over the iridescence
> of horsepiss after rain. Knives, bombs, scandal
> and cowdung fall on women in wedding lace:
> I say nothing, I take care not to gloat. (79)

The poet compares the rot in the Indian mind to horsedung. He compares the Indian in the presence of evil symbolised by the objects of destruction like bombs, knives and scandal, to soft wedding lace on which nothing can make an impact because of its softness. Insensitivity has developed to such an extent that external stimuli have no effect on the deadened sensibilities. The poet is neither depressed nor elated, he is merely indifferent.

> I've learned to watch lovers without envy
> as I'd watch in a bazaar lens
> houseflies rub legs or kiss. I look at wounds calmly. (79)

The poet is incapable of experiencing even the negative emotion of envy. Lovers are degraded to the image of houseflies. His background is such that he is able to look at the suffering around him with as much interest as a disembodied object. Ramanujan, in this poem, speaks about the sensibilities of the average Indian.

> Yet when I meet on a little boy's face
> the prehistoric yellow eyes of a goat
> I choke, for ancient hands are at my throat. (79)

The movement of the poem is from general to specific emotion. The poet experiences agonising emotion only when he sees the innocence in a small boy being smothered by the folds of tradition. The persona is caught in a tradition which has degraded the ideal of non-attachment to indifference.

Though the poet's sensibility is characterised by indifference, yet when there is a confrontation between tradition and modernity, he succumbs to the allure of Western modes. The poem 'Still Another View of Grace' dramatizes the conflict between the two sets of values. As this poem has been discussed in detail the previous chapter, it is not necessary to go into it again. It is sufficient to say that the poet succumbs to the attractiveness of Western values, even though his Brahmin ancestry rebelled against it at first.

Though occasionally he falls a victim to this seduction, he is very ambivalent to Western values, and asserts that he has to work out his salvation in terms of his own tradition. The basic problem of Ramanujan is that he is caught in a cross cultural context. In the poem 'Conventions of Despair,' this problem is dramatised.

> Yes, I know all that. I should be modern.
> Marry again. See strippers at the Tease.
> Touch Africa. Go to the movies.
> Impale a six-inch spider
> Under a lens. Join the test-
> ban or become The Outsider. (34)

To regain his identity, he knows that he has to be modern. The symbol of modernity is to marry again, to have no inhibitions. Modernity is also equated with experimental knowledge. This is suggested by the image of impaling a six-inch spider under a lens. It could also indicate the divorce of science from humanism. Joining the Test-ban means participation in group activities where there is a loss of individual identity. All these images are suggestive of the sterility of modern life.

> Or pay to shake my fist
> (or whatever-you-call-it) at a psychoanalyst.
> And when I burn
> I should smile, dry-eyed,
> and nurse martinis like the Marginal Man. (34)

There is no way of removing neuroses except by paying. This is the dismal condition of the modern man. He has to suppress his desires in drink. The social norms to which the Marginal Man conforms provide him with no outlet for the release of his inhibitions.

Till this point, the poet speaks about conforming to the Western point of view, which is equated with modernity.

> But sorry, I cannot unlearn
> conventions of despair.
> They have their pride.
> I must seek and will find
> my particular hell only in my hindu mind:
> must translate and turn
> till I blister and roast
> for certain lives to come, 'eye-deep,'
> in those boiling crates of oil; weep
> iron tears for winning what I should have lost. (34)

The poet cannot accept Western values. In the West too, people are left with despair in spite of their technical triumphs. The eventual condition of every thinking mind is despair. The poet as it is, experiences the 'particular hell' his Hindu mind has brought him. He sees no valid reason to exchange one kind of despair for another. Ramanujan's poetry is rooted in the tradition of being

Indian. After an endless quest, the conclusion he arrives at is that he has to establish his roots only in terms of the tradition to which he belongs. Ramanujan's search for roots is representative of a similar search perceptible in the poetry of Ezekiel, Parthasarathy and Kamala Das.

According to Indian belief, translation of a language is heresy. But this is precisely what Ramanujan does and he affirms that he will be punished for it. On discovering that Western tradition is inadequate, that writing in English is a sterile occupation, he seeks to resolve his dilemma by translating works in Kannada and Tamil into English. But ironically, though he does win prestige in the West, it is meaningless because translations are sterile. He sheds 'iron tears' for gaining something which he should have lost.

In his fantasy, the poet was a knight, seeking to conquer the West by gaining prestige and becoming rational. But he discovers it is not enough. He realises now that his 'dream-dark queens' have been replaced by 'frog-eyed dragons.' The poet wanted his being to be a mingling of two cultures, of Western rationality and Eastern emotion. But he was saddled with the 'frog-eyed dragons' of Western rationality.

The poem concludes with the poet stating that if he has to see 'through the hole of a stare' his 'Grandchild bare/her teenage flesh to the pimps/of ideal Tomorrow's crowfoot eyes/and the theory of a peacock feathered future,' he had rather endure his present 'Conventions of Despair.' If he had to sacrifice his integrity in the illusion of attaining a falsely attractive future, he would prefer to conform to the 'archaic despair' of his tradition.

The quest for identity, and a usable past, whether spiritual or cultural, a recurrent theme in Indian English poetry, is given a new twist in Ramanujan's *The Black Hen*, a collection of selected poems published posthumously in 1995. In *The Black Hen*, the search for a definite cultural identity is often posited through the use of a text that seeks to re-instate, re-write and revise native idioms and histories, mythologies and local traditions within the context of a larger cultural tradition. Such an ideological perspective transcends ordinary moments in space and time. Through these poems, Ramanujan attempts to establish the authenticity of a cultural and individual identity that is articulated through the language of the metaphysical and the mystical. The visionary quality of *The Black Hen* is used to dramatise a re-interpretation of myth, art and philosophy leading to a reinstatement of the individual self within a larger cultural context.

Modern literary criticism is done with scientific precision, and is devoid of the human experience that the reader brings to the book he is reading. However, we cannot ignore the fact that it is the historicity or the sense of the past that every work of literature carries with it that contextualises it and makes it the carrier of its own unique aesthetic experience.

Seen in this light, it is the context that determines the cultural tradition to which the text belongs. It is interesting to observe that in *The Black Hen* written between 1989 and 1993, the poems go beyond the regressive quality of a static tradition. "Texts," in the words of Edward Said, "are wordily, to some degree they are events, and, even when they appear to deny it, they are nevertheless a part of the social world, human life, and of course the historical moments in which they are located and interpreted."[3]

In the earlier volumes, Ramanujan's concern had been confined to the particular—to his family, his relations, his Indian past, and to a common heritage. The familial experience is linked with a historical consciousness. The nostalgic tone of Ramanujan's earlier poetry is the collective nostalgia of a whole people who look back and attempt to find comfort in a 'communal past.' The present, in the wake of Westernization loosely equated with modernization, is only an amalgam of disintegration. The once stable values now give way under the onslaught of Westernization. The images in most of the earlier poems reveal the stagnation of the poet's culture. Without the strong foundation of culture and tradition, the life of the thinly disguised persona in these poems is sterile, as is the life around him.

But in *The Black Hen,* the sterility of his culture finds acceptance in poems that deal with death, decay, nihilism and other self-annihilating factors. The tradition to which the persona belongs is now identified with the aridness of modern experience that was exemplified in all its painful intensity in T.S. Eliot's *The Waste Land.* The twentieth century theory of logical positivism and scientific materialism brought about an intellectual sterility that sought ineffectively to define the meaning and purpose of existence.

In the poem 'The Black Hen,' (which is the first poem in this posthumous collection), the artist's compulsive desire to create is subverted to express states of negation. Poetry is no longer 'emotion recollected in tranquillity.' Poetry must come "as leaves/to a tree/or not at all," and when it does, it shocks and stuns. Poetic creation is a laborious process and it comes 'sometimes/as the black hen/with the red round eye/on the embroidery/stitch by stitch/dropped and found again/and when it's all there/ the black hen stares/with its round red eye/and you're afraid.' (195) The startling richness of the colour imagery suggests satanic overtones. The *black* hen with the *red* round eye, activates, not very gently, an oppressive consciousness of the past, a disillusioned awareness of the present and maybe a depressing uncertainty about the future. The larger cultural tradition of a social reality that is formidable and complex, from which one cannot escape as the word 'stare' suggests, appears to be the cause of this unconscious fear. If art reflects life, then art is that which imposes a credible form on reality. It introduces a pattern of order on a seeming mass of contradictions which define the basic experience of existence.

In these later poems, Ramanujan chose certain voices, images and metaphors to articulate his concept of nature and culture. His view of culture transcends the earlier limited concept of an Indian tradition. 'Foundlings on the Yukon' is centred on an actual incident in the Yukon territory in Northern Canada, one of the coldest inhabited regions on earth. A group of miners discovered some seeds "sealed off by a landslide." Out of this 'six grains were whole.' They were picked and planted 'ten thousand/years after their time/they took root,' and within forty-eight hours, sprouted eight small leaves, 'having skipped/a million falls/ . . . by an accident of flowering.' (196) These saplings were the upstarts of a modern age, greedy and ambitious, self-serving and self-centred.

In 'Shadows,' the strategy of parody is employed to link the text and the context with a culture that is regressive and sterile. In this world, 'shadows fall between people/when they walk in the sun,' 'women circumambulate the peepul/tree hoping for a son,' and 'war heroes return in special trains/Covered with blood and flags.' (199) In 'Bosnia,' the poet writes: 'How can one write about Bosnia/Biafra, Bangladesh just to take/only the atrocities that begin with B?" (247) The bleakness of contemporary society is reflected in 'At Zero.' In Indian philosophy, the concept of zero was first propounded by the Buddhist philosopher, Nagarjuna. His aim was to show that nothing positive or negative can be asserted as reality. It is therefore, *shunya,* or *zero*, or vacuity or emptiness. But even to think of reality as *shunya* is a mistake because the concepts of emptiness and vacuity are understood with reference to fullness. *Shunya* is beyond all opposites and contradictions, and is symbolically associated with *nirvana* or the ultimate spiritual goal. *Shunya,* that is, zero, is neither positive nor negative. Yet we cannot say it has no value. It makes an infinite series of positive numbers, and an equally infinite series of negative numbers possible. Zero is used to mean not only *shunya* but also *purna* (fullness). But in 'At Zero,' this metaphysical truth is inverted to generate only a series of negations, because 'at zero,' every kind of object, whether inanimate, dead, or still living is permeated with a deadening stillness. The images range surreally from 'clocks losing their tongues' with their still pendulums likened to the scrotums of dead bulls, to 'blank Brahmin-widow faces,' and a plane poised to take off into nowhere, for 'the eye looks,/cannot see anything/but currents of vapor/curling/in the transparency." (200) In 'Zero' the persona narrates, 'zero has no value until it follows a real number/he said,/like you, me, and this talk/ I said." (263)

In 'Salamanders,' the same idea of nothingness is elaborated. 'Again, here it comes, the nothing, /the zero where numbers die or begin./ . . . where sounds do not become words/nor words the rivals of silence." (202) In 'Fog,' the Self struggles to emerge from a 'swirl/of fog that lifts an hour at a time,/a cold that burns without blisters,/pulse ticking off time like/an umpire over a fallen wrestler." (208) There appears to be no hope for either renewal or regeneration of the human spirit.

In 'In March,' the journey of the Self acquires surreal and mystical overtones. The journey is allegorically set within the blood stream of the body. This journey reveals the savagery and violence of the psychic disorders that lurk within the depths of the unconscious. 'The alligators' with 'their rows of sharp teeth,' 'the red-hot fish' that circled his continents through 'the stillness of icebergs/and sleepless oceans' were insignificant in the face of the horrific realization that 'I never knew that my Amazon/ flows savage and treacherous/through my Africas.' (238)

The visionary quality of 'In March' is extended to 'A Meditation.' This poem embodies the multiplicity of one's being evident in a fragmented consciousness. The speaker imagines his aging body as a black walnut tree. The tree is exposed to nature's depredations, and finally, it lies uprooted in a storm. The municipality 'cut it up in convenient/pieces.' The Carpenter made a butcher's block table and a butcher's block chair, the paper factory turned its bark and leaves into rolls of paper. The speaker finally imagines himself sitting, 'and as I write/I know I'm writing now on my head/now on my torso, my living/hands moving/ on a dead one.' (239) The human consciousness itself is a product that is split, processed, and distributed by the dictates of a materialist society. The unconscious, which is impervious to conscious criticism and control, is perhaps, the one area that is defenseless and vulnerable to all kinds of perverse influences. In 'No Fifth Man,' poetry, which symbolically articulates the nature of the unconscious, is compared to a tigress that 'takes your breath away' when it exposes your vulnerability to a marauding world. (243)

In a series of poems entitled 'Mythologies I,' 'Mythologies 2' and 'Mythologies 3,' the poet employs the technique of using Indian Myths to articulate this panic. In 'Mythologies I' he uses the myth of Puttanna and states, 'O terror with a baby face, /suck me dry, Drink my venom/Renew my breath..' (221) In 'Mythologies 2,' he pleads with Vishnu, to 'End my commerce with bat and night-owl.' (226) In 'Mythologies 3,' he resorts to the legend of Mahadeviyakka to articulate his yearning for a vision of Lord Shiva who is equated with spiritual illumination. (228)

The re interpretation of myth, art and philosophy that form the basic motif of *The Black Hen* is a testimony to the disintegrating values of our times. But *The Black Hen* also offers a redemptive vision. Appropriately enough, the last poem is called 'Fear No Fall.' It was written on 11 April, 1993, shortly before the poet's death. It tells the story of Arunagiri, 'a truant extraordinary,/escape artist, burglar of hearts,' 'unlettered and worthless' who 'hated temple bells and hypocrisies.' (275) In a vision he is told to sing of Murugan by an 'Old Man' who gave him his first line of verse. The spiritual transformation of the wayward Arunagiri into a saint was expressed in his devotional songs that ensnared passers by, 'unlocking cages/even for mynahs and parrots.' The poet's spiritual dilemma appears to dissolve as he feels that he too may be redeemed by a Voice which averts his fear of 'falling . . . in the gutters below' by calling out to him both within and without, 'Fall, fall,/you'll never fear a fall again,/fall now!' (275)

In *The Black Hen*, Eastern and Western culture blend to create an ethical imagination which introduces a dimension of depth into an otherwise parodic play of empty imitation. Poetry, when combined with ethical sensibility, opens a whole new dimension of positive interpretation by releasing a pluri-dimensionality of meaning. As in Eliot's *The Waste Land*, in Ramanujan's Poetry too, the search for an integrating principle moves on several diverging planes—that of autobiography, mythology, religion, legend, and belief. Ultimately, it is the strength and validity of spiritual wisdom over mere scientific knowledge that can lead to the realisation of an integrated spiritual self. In this waste land, as in Eliot's poem, until the thunder resounds, and the rain descends, there can only be the perpetuity of nothingness and an endless wait for divine benediction. One's natural desire for conceptual knowledge has to be renounced in favour of a non-conceptual knowledge that could lead to a whole new mode of knowing and loving in this spiritual waste land. To Ramanujan, it perhaps lay in an unconditional surrender to God.

Through these poems, Ramanujan projects the deepest fears and desires of an alienated self. Writing has always been considered as a mode of establishing one's identity. Ramanujan's personal quest for identity transcends the limits of a limited cultural context. The psychic predicament he articulates in his text is a universal one. The multi-cultural transformation, that crystallises into a reinstatement of the individual self within a definite universal cultural context in *The Black Hen*, goes beyond a resurgence of the merely traditional and essentialist statement of cultural origin and identity.

In recent times, cross-culturation has resulted in new levels of influence that transcend earlier notions of national identity and culture. Contemporary texts have often used subjects that are not immediately connected with their own social or political issues, or questions of identity, to rework into their own canon the complex multiplicity of cross-cultural relationships. *The Black Hen* by recognising syncreticity is thus a re-inscription of new universal and cultural 'realities,' and the means to come to terms with it.

References

1 Devindra Kohli, "Indian Poetry in English: Two Views," *The Journal of Common Wealth Literature*, Vol. IX, No. 1, ed. Arthur Ravenscroft (Leeds: Oxford Univ. Press, 1974), p. 29.

2 *The Collected poems of A.K. Ramanujan* (Delhi: Oxford University Press, 1995), p. 23. All further references to this text are indicated by page numbers in parenthesis.

3 Edward W. Said, *The World, The Text and the Critic* (London: Vintage, 1991), p. 4.

Chapter IV

A Comparative Study of the Poetry and Translations of A.K. Ramanujan

In these four volumes of poetry, Ramanujan's deep awareness of Indian myths and legends, Indian history, her varied customs and rituals, her philosophy, and her way of life is amply evident. As an expatriate, this overwhelming concern with his Indian past speaks of an intellect and a soul that is extricably bound and sustained by a tradition that is enriching and fulfilling. Though proficient in both Tamil, his mother tongue, and Kannada, the language he grew up with and studied, his poems were predominantly written in English. Ramanujan's translations of classical Tamil poetry, and the Kannada *Vacanas* in English helped to propagate Tamil and Kannada in the West. Speaking of his poetic art, Ramanujan remarked, "English and my disciplines [linguistics, anthropology] give me my 'outer' forms—linguistic, metrical, logical and other such ways of shaping experience; and my first thirty years in India, my frequent visits and field trips, my personal and professional pre-occupations with Kannada, Tamil, the classics and folklore give me my substance, my 'inner' forms, images and symbols."[1]

The Indian believes that his mind is a vast storehouse of ideas, images, and archetypes. These *samskaras* constantly increase the contents of one's consciousness. They are an inherent part of it, and it is to these that the poet appeals through language. In the light of Ramanujan's own admission regarding his indebtedness to Kannada, Tamil, the Indian classics, and the Indian folklore for giving him the 'inner' forms, images and symbols of his poetry, it would be interesting to study and comparatively assess Ramanujan's original creative work as a poet in

English with his translations in English of Tamil and Kannada poetry in terms of structural, thematic and linguistic parallels blending together the historical, formalistic, and socio-realistic approaches. Such an assessment would develop the ability to read literature critically, and acquire a broader sense of literary tradition and history. It would enable one to indicate and study affinity, tradition, or influence between the translated works on one hand, and the original creative work on the other. This would lead to an investigation regarding the possibility of continuities and parallels in terms of thematics as well as structures. It would also engender a study of cross-cultural movements and trends that can influence literary studies.

Since Ramanujan was a poet in English too, the chief objective would be to critically evaluate whether his translated poems affected his creativity as a poet through a practical analysis of his works. The objective would be to demonstrate through practical criticism whether with each new translator his poetic sensibility, the current poetic idioms, as well as the prevailing ethical political notions influence his works. If this is the case, then, is there the possibility of arriving at an 'inner form,' a 'fidelity' or 'a structure' that may well influence the writer's creativity as a poet? Therefore, is translation transcreation, or *deutero creative* where the critic asserts that the supreme critical act is not evaluation but recognition? Ramanujan has more than often been assessed as an Indian poet writing in English. But he remains perhaps the greatest translator that India has ever produced in modern times. His translations of poetry in English have seldom, if at all, been compared with his original, creative writings. When a person is both a translator and a poet in the same language, i.e., English, there are bound to be certain inferences, similarities and parallels. Does being a translator affect the creativity demanded by a poet? Such a study can re-define the notion of creativity involved in translating poetry, and writing poetry in the same language. New creative contexts require new critical accents which should balance the modern with the indigenous.

This comparative analysis is conceived as a part of this quest for a usable past in terms of aesthetic categories.

Ramanujan's books of translations are: *Fifteen Poems from a Classical Tamil Anthology* (1965), *The Interior Landscape* (1967), *Lotus in the Navel* (1969), *Speaking of Siva* (1972), *Samskara* (1976), *Hymns for the Drowning* (1981), *Poems of Love and War* (1985). My main concern would be to analyse his translations of Tamil poetry as found in *The Interior Landscape*, *Poems of Love and War*, *Hymns for the Drowning*, and to a certain extent his translations of the Kannada *Vacanas* in *Speaking of Siva.*

The art of formal translation has been traced back to 3000 B.C by literary historians. Apparently Emperor Sargoan of Assyria declared that his heroic exploits should be translated into all the Assyrian languages so that all the people of Assyria would be informed of his glory. This appears to be the first attempt at formal translation. Translation appears to have been an interesting pre-occupation with the Romans too. They were so inspired by their neighbours, the Greeks, that they translated as many of their literary works into Latin as they could. In the West, form and order was given to the process of translation through the rendering of the Bible. The Bible was originally written in Hebrew that was little understood by many. Translations of the Bible were literal, and only the bare meaning was preferred. Translations of other texts into English began in England in the ninth century by King Alfred. He translated a number of Latin texts into English. His objective was to lessen the insular solitude of the island by exposing his people to fresh thoughts, ideas, and insights. Translation for him was the creation of a vernacular text that would develop national consciousness. However, till the fourteenth century, English was regarded as a corrupt language fit only for translations. It was only in the fifteenth century that England came into the golden age of prose translations. William Caxton, and Thomas Malory enriched the English language with their translations of popular romances from the French, Latin, and Dutch. The English translation of Sir Thomas More's *Utopia* in 1551 is regarded as a masterpiece of English Humanism. In the field of translations of poetry, Wyatt (1503-42) and Surrey's (1517-47) *Tottel*'s *Miscellany* was published posthumously in 1557. Chapman's *Homer* was published in 1616. Translation was not confined to mere paraphrase now. Stylistic details were given a lot of importance. The publication of the English Bible exerted the greatest influence on English literature. Its translation began in the eighth century and it continued in various versions till the seventeenth century. It ended in 1611 with the issue of the *King James Bible* or *The Authorised Version*. This is regarded as one of the greatest works of English translations. The eighteenth and nineteenth century again witnessed a remarkable development in the field of translation. Pope's translation of the *Iliad* and *Odyssey* are important developments. But he deviated too much from the original, and earned the comment: "It is a pretty poem, Mr. Pope, but you must not call it Homer."[2] But Johnson praised Pope's *Iliad* and said, "It is certainly the noblest version of poetry that the world has ever seen."[3] In 1859, Edward Fitzgerald's English translation of Omar Khayyam from Persian changed the concept of translation. It enjoyed great popularity, but one critic, Fitz Maurice Kelly remarked: "by a miracle of intrepid dexterity, a half-forgotten Persian poet is transfigured into a pessimistic English genius."[4]

It was Dryden in the seventeenth century who laid the basis for the English translation theory. Dryden broadly defined translation as metaphrase, paraphrase, and imitation. In the preface to Ovid's *Epistles*, he wrote, "First that of metaphrase or turning an author word by word, and line by line, from one language into another . . . the second way is that of paraphrase, or translation with latitude where the author is kept in view by the translator, so as never to be lost, but his words are not so strictly followed as his sense, and that too is admitted to be amplified, but not altered . . . the third way is imitation, where the translator (if now he has not lost that name) assumes the liberty not only to vary from the words and sense, but to forsake them both as he sees the occasion, and taking only some general hints from the original to run division on the ground-work, as he pleases."[5]

It was Dryden's firm conviction that the translator should not attempt to better the original. However, his practice in translation gave him the knowledge that only a poet can truly understand and reveal another poet. He later took liberties with his own translation, his aim being the attainment of greater aesthetic impact than freedom. He translated Juvenal, Ovid, Virgil and practised all modes of translation such as metaphrase, paraphrase, and imitation. He realised, however, that imbuing a work with life was more important than defining its outline literally. Two opposing views on translation prevailed during the period. One group held that the translator should improve and embellish the original, while the other group demanded that the translator should be strictly literal in his translations, translating even the flaws and defects of the original. Debate on these two issues went on for a long time.

In the latter half of the twentieth century, J.C. Catford and Eugene A. Nida dominated the field. Catford emphasized the significance of meaning in the process of translation, and spoke about the 'formal' relations and the 'contextual' relations which are entered into by the units of a language. He dealt with phonological translation, graphological translation, grammatical translation, lexical translation and transliteration. He gave a sound linguistic basis to translation studies.

Eugene A. Nida's works analysed the process of translation minutely. He stated: "Translating consists in producing in the RL the closest natural equivalent to the message of the source language, first in meaning and secondly in style."[6] It recognised for the first time the lack of any absolute correspondence. At the same time he pointed out the necessity of finding the closest equivalent. He stressed that translation is essentially a process of communication which involves two languages. Besides, language has to be considered along with its essential relationship to the cultural context as a whole. In him theory and practice converge.

In recent times, nearly all translation studies uphold the right of the translation to be different from the original. A creative writer is expected to give his own interpretation of a literary work in a medium which is similar to but different from the medium of that of the original. This leads to the concept of transcreation. The essence and spirit of the translated work is more important than a mere transliteration.

In the literary tradition of India, translation has been chiefly considered as 'New writing' rather than an imitation of the original work. This could be because in India the literary tradition of writing commentaries on the *Gita*, the *Upanishads,* or of translating tales from the *Ramayana* and the *Mahabharata* continued for centuries. For instance Pampa's *Mahabharat* in Kannada, or Kadamba's *Ramayan* in Tamil are considered as original works, though they do contain the thematic and narrative imitations of the original. Translations of classical works into English began with the advent of the British in India. Since Sanskrit literature had the monopoly of being termed classical for many centuries, most of the translations were from Sanskrit into English. Early religious compositions in Tamil also attracted translations into English. The earliest translation from Sanskrit to English was William Jones' *Sacoontala* published in 1789 from Calcutta. Early translations emphasized fidelity to the original "making allowances only for the unavoidable lexical or linguistic, cultural or environmental adjustments with the original."[7] "The notion that every literary translation is a faithful rendering of the original came to us from the West, perhaps in the wake of the Bible and need felt by Christian missionaries to have it translated into different Indian languages."[8] The translator of modern works cannot take liberties with the original text as the translators of ancient and mediaeval texts because he is not separated in time and space from the original author as those translators are. The translator of relatively modern works enjoys a double readership—of the original work as well as of the translated work.

Early Indian translators followed the Indian concept of 'anuvada' or adaptation, rather than a literal rendering of the original text into the target language. Until the advent of Western culture in India, India had always regarded translation as New Writing. Texts were often re-told or re-made by authors to suit their own purposes. In the West, translation moved either from extreme fidelity to the original, or to utter freedom from the original. In India, modern translations were influenced by the West, but it did not maintain the sharp distinction Western literature generally made between original writing and writing derived from other texts. *Rupantar* (meaning 'change in form') and *anuvad* ('speaking after' or 'following') is the definition of translation in India, and neither demands fidelity to the original. The efficacy of a translation will depend, as the *Authorized Version* of the *Bible* in English proves, on the extent of its "appropriation into the translator's own language, and the degree of its domestication into the translator's own culture."[9] For the Indian translator in English this is a major problem. While controlling the English language (as in the case of A.K. Ramanujan) with an appreciable degree of competence may be possible, it is the degree of its domestication into the translator's own culture that might be problematic. Sujit Mukherjee remarks, "If it is accepted that any act of translation means the naturalization by transfer of an alien quantity, the Indian translator is involved in transferring an Indian (native) text through a non-Indian language such as English (alien) into the Indian culture (native)" while his English counterpart is "transferring an Indian text (alien) through his native language into his native culture."[10] Such a process has been lately called transcreation, especially for rendering older literary texts into modern English. This term was advocated by P. Lal, the poet-translator-publisher at Calcutta. In his introductory note to his version of *Shakuntala*, he says, "Faced by such a variety of material, the translator must edit, reconcile and transmute; his job in many ways becomes largely a matter of transcreation."[11] Transcreation, instead of involving wide departures from the original, is to him, the closest to the original. This again can be disputed because "of the likely variations between the translator's understanding and the critic's understanding of the original, between the translator's intended re-statement in transcreation and the critic's achieved reading of the re-statement."[12] However, the object of all translations is, as George Steiner says, at its best, the peculiar synthesis of conflict and complicity between a poem and its translation into another poem creating the impression of a "third language," of a medium of communicative energy which somehow reconciles both languages in a tongue deeper, more comprehensive than the other."[13]

Ramanujan's interest in translation began in the year 1962. In the Translator's Note to *Poems of Love and War* from the *Eight Anthologies and the Ten Long Poems of Classical Tamil*, he states, "Even one's own tradition is not one's birthright. It has to be earned, repossessed. . . . One chooses and translates a part of one's past to make it present to oneself. One comes face to face with it sometimes in faraway places as I did. In 1962 on one of my first Saturdays in the University of Chicago, I entered the basement stacks of the then Harper library in search of an elementary grammar of Old Tamil, which I never learned. The University had just acquired a vast collection of books from a famous south Indian historian. . . . As I searched . . . I came upon an early anthology of classical Tamil poems, edited in 1937 by U.Ve. Caminataiyar. It carried his Tamil signature, dated 1937, on its flyleaf. That edition, I later learned, was a landmark in its own right. I sat down on the floor between the stacks and began to browse. To my amazement, I found the prose commentary transparent; it soon unlocked the old poems for me. As I began to read on, I was enthralled by the beauty and subtlety of what I could read. Here was a world, a part of my language and culture, to which I had been an ignorant heir."[14] Ramanujan subsequently translated into English the poems that appear in this Anthology. Ramanujan had this to say about his translations, "Dancers and composers have translated my translations further into their own arts. . . . The ancient poets composed in Tamil for their Tamil corner of the world of antiquity; but, as nothing human is alien, they have reached ages unborn and 'accents yet unknown.' I am grateful, and astonished, to be one of the links, undreamed of by them or me."[15]

To Ramanujan, to translate is to "carry across." Translations are transpositions; and some elements of the original cannot be transposed at all. For instance, "one can often convey a sense of the original rhythm but not the language-bound meter; one can mimic levels of diction, even the word-play, but not the actual sound of the words. Items are more difficult to translate than relations, textures more difficult than structure, words more difficult than phrasing, linear order more difficult than syntax, lines more difficult than pattern. Yet poetry is made at all those levels—and so is translation."[16] Ramanujan attempts to approximate Dryden's definition of translation "to keep as near my author as I could, without losing all his graces, the most eminent of which are in the beauty of his words; and those words, I must add, are always figurative . . . taking all the materials of this divine author, I have endeavoured to make [him] speak such English as he himself would have spoken . . . in this present age."[17]

Ramanujan further stated that when two languages are as startlingly different from each other as modern English and mediaeval Tamil, the task of translation appears to be even more daunting. "The 'left-branching' syntax of Tamil is most often a reverse mirror image of the possible English. Mediaeval Tamil is written with no punctuation, and no spaces between words; it has neither articles nor prepositions, and the words are 'agglutinative,' layered with suffixes. The syntax is a dense embedding of clause within clause. I translate unit by syntactic unit and try to recreate the way the parts articulate the poem in the original. My English thus seems to occupy more visual space on the page than the adjective-packed, participle-crowded Tamil original. The 'sound-look,' the syntax, the presence or absence of punctuation and the sequential design are part of the effort to bring the Tamil poems faithfully to an English reader."[18]

Ramanujan continues, "Though only poems can translate poems, a translator is 'an artist on oath.' He has a double allegiance, indeed several double allegiances. All too familiar with the rigors and pleasures of reading a text, and those of making another, caught between the need to express himself and the need to represent another . . . he has to use both to get close to 'the originals.' He has to let poetry win without allowing scholarship to lose. Then his very compromises may begin to express a certain fidelity, and may suggest what he cannot convey. Crossing languages, one ancient or foreign, another current and familiar, searching in one language for forms and tones that will mimic and relive those of another, he may fashion now and then a third that will look like the one and speak like (or for) the other. Yet, more often than not, his task, like Marvell's love is "begotten by despair upon impossibility."[19]

In the Introduction to his first book of Tamil translations from the Tamil Sangam poetry, *The Interior Landscape*, Ramanujan wrote, "Anyone translating a poem into a foreign language is at the same time trying to translate the foreign reader into a native one."[20] It was a method by which he entered into the soul of a poem, repossessing it, and making it his own. Translation is the result of admiration, and admiration entails a certain humility while translating. So translation has to be close to the original. Ramanujan's basic response was to the structure of the poem. By breaking up lines and arranging them in little units and paragraphs or arranging them step-wise, he attempted to arrive at a visual shape which would indicate the shape of the original.

The term 'inner form,' 'fidelity' and 'structure' might indicate that Ramanujan's aim was to keep the translator aloof from his translated work. But objectivity did not mean a 'correct' rendering of the text. Indeed this was not so. The choices that the translator made was in consonance with the needs and desires of his innermost soul or personality. Ramanujan states, "A translation has to be true to the translator no less than to the original. He cannot jump off his shadow. Translation is a choice, interpretation, an assertion of taste, a betrayal of what answers one's needs."[21] This statement acquires tremendous significance in the light of his own original poetic creativity. Surely his translations were chosen deliberately to fit into his secular, sophisticated outlook. By analysing the structure and themes of his Tamil translations, it is possible to arrive at an interesting conclusion. By Ramanujan's own admission, he 'rediscovered' and 'repossessed' his Tamil tradition through his readings and translations of select Tamil poetry: If the mind is a storehouse of archetypes and primordial images, then it might be justifiable to admit a certain measure of influence that these translations exerted over his 'Originality' and Creativity as a poet in English. Girish Karnad remarks: "Ramanujan himself believed that with each new translator his poetic sensibility, the current poetic idioms, as well as the prevailing ethical-political notions must all come into play."[22] A poet expresses himself when he is deeply affected by certain perceptions. A translator chooses certain works to be translated deliberately. It could be because he finds a deep affinity for the work he is translating. His work does not stop at a mere rendering of the linguistic and textual structure of the poem. The repossessing entails a capturing of the essence or soul of the translated work. This essence couched in current poetic idioms, or the prevailing ethical-political notion pervades the entire range of Ramanujan's poems in English.

Ramanujan's concern has been to render a poem phrase by phrase, instead of line by line, as each phrase articulates the total poem. The Tamil poets had no capitals, punctuation marks, nor any regular end-rhymes in the kind of blank verse they used for all their poems. Tamil, unlike English, has a 'free word-order.' The poets made excellent use of this freedom to create their poetic forms; the central nuance of a poem is most often enacted by the unusual yet perfectly acceptable positioning of sentence-parts, and by the strategic placing of "insets" of imagery. The visual shapes of the poems are not arbitrary or eccentric. They indicate the design of the original poems, and are an essential part of the attempt at fidelity. A dense adjective-packed, participle-crowded Tamil poem may become in Ramanujan's English a piece of ten lines. He says, "I have had to choose between transplanting the physical look of Tamil lines and transposing their patterned internal syntax, and I have invariably chosen the latter course."[23]

In *Poems of Love and War*, Ramanujan translates old Tamil poems selected from anthologies compiled over two millennia ago. The poems in this book are selected from the *Eight Anthologies* and *The Ten Long Poems*; sections of the Tolkappiyam are used to develop a commentary on Tamil poetry and poetics. The poems are classified by their themes as *akam* and *puram*. *Akam* meant 'interior" and *puram* 'exterior.' *Akam* poems were love poems; *Puram* poems were poems on war. The selections here have one book of *akam* poems, and another of *puram*. The *akam* poems are presented in five sections. Each section contains poems that evoke a particular landscape: hillside, seaside, forests, cultivated fields, and the wilderness (or desert). Each landscape with the mood it represents, and the poems that evoke it, is called by the name of a flower or plant of that region: *Kurinci*, a mountain flower; *neytal*, blue lily; *mullai,* jasmine; *marutam,* queen's flower; *palai*, a desert tree. In *puram* poems, certain situations (ex. a siege), persons (ex. a chieftain), and themes (ex. ideals of good life) appear to be more important than landscapes. So Ramanujan has arranged these poems under five themes. Kings at War, Poets and Dancers, Chieftain's Lessons, War and After.

The third and fourth books consist of a few late classical poems (fifth to sixth century) with a different subject. The third offers some comic, even bawdy poems, poems of love's excess in contrast to the decorum of the previous sections. The fourth and last book includes a long hymn to Vishnu, one of the earliest examples of its kind in Indian literature, and two pieces from the long poem, "A Guide to Lord Murukan." The erotic and heroic motifs of *akam* and *puram* are imaginatively reworked in these early important religious poems.[24]

In the *akam* poems, the characters are limited by convention to a small number: the hero, the heroine, the hero's friend(s) or messengers, the heroine's friend and foster mother, the concubine, and the passerby. No poet here speaks in his own voice, and no poem is addressed to a reader. The reader only overhears what the characters say to each other, to themselves, or to the moon. A poem in this tradition implies, evokes and enacts a drama in a monologue. In the *akam* poems, the titles are therefore 'What She Said,' 'What He Said,' 'What Her Friend Said,' 'What the Foster Mother Said,' 'What Her Friend Said to Him,' 'What Her Girl-Friend Said to Her' and 'What Her Girl-Friend Said to the Unfaithful Husband.'

Akam poetry concerns itself with "the middle five" phases or types of love and outlines their symbolic conventions. There are four kinds of "Place," and each is presided over by a deity, and named for a flower or tree characteristic of the region.

> *Mullai,* a variety of Jasmine, stands for the forests overseen by Mayon, the dark-bodied God of herdsmen;
>
> *Kurinci,* a mountain flower, for the mountains overseen by Murukan, the red-speared god of war, youth and beauty.
>
> *Marutam*, a tree with red flowers growing near the water, for the pastoral region, overseen by Ventan, the rain god.
>
> *Neytal*, a water flower, for the sandy sea shore overseen by the wind god;
>
> *Palai* or desert waste has no specific location. It is named after *palai,* supposedly an evergreen tree unaffected by drought. It is overseen by *Korravai*, a demonic goddess of war.
>
> *Mullai* country is associated with the rainy season and evening. *Kurinci* with the early frost and midnight; *Marutam* with the later part of night and dawn; *Neytal* with the twilight of evening; *Palai* with summer, late frost and midday.

Each of the five regions or landscapes is associated further with an appropriate *Uri,* or human feeling associated with a phase of love. For instance, lovers' union is associated with *kurinci,* the mountains; separation with *palai*, the desert; patient waiting with *mullai,* the forests; anxious waiting with *neytal*, the sea-shore; the lover's infidelity and resentment with *marutam*, the pastoral region. Each landscape has its native elements (*karu*): gods, foods, animals, trees, birds, drums, occupations, lutes, or musical styles and such others. Flowers and kinds of running or standing water are also added.

Each phase of love gets its characteristic types of imagery from a particular landscape. Flowers like *mullai* and *kurinci* are names not only of landscapes but of the associated feeling, and of the type of poetry devoted to them. Thus each of these landscapes is used to symbolize and evoke a specific feeling.[25] The objective landscape of Tamil country becomes the interior landscape of Tamil poetry. The 'Interior' world is archetypal. It has no history and no names of persons and places, except now and then, in its metaphors. Love in all its variety is the theme of *akam*. There are seven types of love. The first is *kaikillai* or unrequited love, and the last is *peruntinai* or mismatched love. This is a forced and loveless relationship between a man and a woman. But of the seven types of love, only the middle five are the subject of true love poetry.

An analysis of the following *akam* poem can illustrate the above statement.

What She Said

As the lovely new flower
    of the small-leaved cow's thorn
covers the meadows
    and gives birth
to thorns
my lover who was kind
now does evil,
    and I'm sick at heart (Allur Nanmullai[26] *Koruntokai*, 202)

This poem belongs to the category of *marutam* or the lover's unfaithfulness after marriage. The speaker and the lover are not named. The speaker seems to be talking to herself, or to a confidante. The deceptive beauty of the little flowers evokes a mood of ironic and sullen comment on the lover's infidelity. The lovely new flowers of the small leaved cow's thorn covers the lowlands as indicated in the term 'meadows.' It is set in the fertile countryside. Inscapes of the natural scene repeat the total action of the poem. An inset is an implicit comparison. Unlike metaphor, in ordinary language, an inset is a structural feature within the poem; it integrates the different elements of the poem and shapes its message. Metonymy, where the signifier and the signified belong to the same universe and share the same landscape, is an important poetic figure of classical Tamil poetry. The Tamil theory of comparison, whether explicit or implicit, includes terms of comparison that refer to shape, color, action, or result. Other points of comparison include comparisons based on touch, taste, etc. In the poem, the lush meadows once symbolic of the joyful union of the lovers, are now covered with the thorns of infidelity, and the beloved is full of despair.

'Puram' means 'exterior, outer parts of the body, yard outside the house, public.' The *Puram* poems correspond to the *akam* poems in many ways. There is a *puram* parallel for every one of the seven genres of *akam.* Though the *akam/puram* correspondences are not strict, they complement one another. They are contrasted in theme, mood and structure, but are unified by imagery. While *akam* poems contain only ideal types in the 'Inner world,' *puram* refers to the public. It is allowed names, places, expression of personal circumstances in a real society, a real history, and a certain freedom from the necessities of poetic convention both in insets and in the landscapes. The meanings complement each other systematically. This is true of Ramanujan's poetry in English. Ramanujan states, "As we move from context to context, for each meaning of *akam*, there is a corresponding sense of *puram.* It is characteristic of this poetry and its poetics that the meanings seem to expand and contract in concentric circles, with the concrete physical particular at the center, getting more and more inclusive and abstract as we move outward. The context picks and foregrounds one or another of these circles of meaning."[27] The poem moves along these various senses of *akam* and *puram.* In the course of such interplay, *akam/puram* contrasts such as inner/outer, self/other, nature/

culture, household/wilderness become part of the poem as well as the context of the poem.[28]

Hymns for the Drowning contain some of the earliest religious poems about Vishnu, or Tirumal, the Dark one. The author is an 'alvar' "(one) immersed in god," the root verb *al* means "to immerse, to dive, to sink, to be lowered, to be deep." The title plays on the meanings of such an immersion for poet and reader. These poems written by Nammalvar between AD 880 to 930 represent the most important early *bhakti* texts in any Indian language. Early *bhakti* movements were devoted to Siva or Vishnu. *Hymns for the Drowning* is chiefly concerned with poems related to Vishnu, and his incarnations. *Speaking of Siva* is a book of *vacanas* or religious lyrics in Kannada free verse. The *vacanas* were written between the tenth and twelfth century in India by the Virasaiva saints. The spontaneity of worship that is characteristic of the *bhakti* movement advocated total surrender to god. In *Speaking of Siva*, Ramanujan translated into English some of the *vacanas* of the four great mystic poets of the period: D Basavanna, Devara Dasimayya, Mahadeviyakka and Allama Prabhu.

Ramanujan's four volumes of English poetry reveal a certain degree of indebtedness to his translations. The methodology used by the Tamil poets in his translation entitled *Poems of Love and War* reveal a correspondence in the structural and thematic design of his poems. Tradition provides a linguistic-cultural landscape in which the issue of identity and roots becomes the major theme of a work of art. The 'collective unconscious' as conveyed through creative expression, can be identified with the help of various parameters such as the linguistic structure, genres and styles, themes, cultural milieu, philosophical vision, ideology and geophysical space (country, region, continent).[29] The content of Ramanujan's poetry is extremely Indian. These poems can be arranged in a particular sequence for interpretive purposes. They resemble the 'Interior Landscape' of Tamil poetry mediating between an individual and the large social world. The *akam* and *puram* definitions of the structure of classical Tamil poetry can be extended to Ramanujan's poetry. In his first two volumes, i.e.

Relations and *Striders*, Ramanujan's pre-occupation is with his family. His social and personal poetry can be interpreted within a series of concentric circles. At the outermost periphery (as in *The Black Hen*) is the representation of various environments that lie on the edge of the poet's experience, while the innermost periphery brings together poems that are closest to him. In the smallest circle, "We come face to face with the poet by himself, as the individual who experiences everything, confronts himself more closely than anything else, and serves as the subjective center which gives all the concentric zones of experience their basic structure and meaning."[30]

His theme is announced in the epigraph poem, a translation from Tamil occurring in the *Poems of Love and War* entitled *Relations*. It is also the title given to his first volume of poems.

Like a hunted deer
on the wide white
salt land,
a flayed hide
turned inside out,
One may run,
escape.
But living
among relations
binds the feet. [31]

The *akam* poems delve into the intricacies of the poet's personal dilemma. In *The Striders*, the alienated persona describes his isolated and self-centered existence (a characteristic of modern existence) through the image of the strider, a water insect. The image is related to his own self, but

This bug sits
on a landslide of lights
and drowns eye
deep
into its tiny strip
of sky (3)

Familial relationships do not bring in any comfort. His sister's hair in 'snakes' metaphorically evokes only sibilant images of hisses, coils and writhing curves recalling feelings of horror and revulsion.

> Sister ties her braids
> with a knot of tassel
> but the weave of her knee-long braid has scales,
> their gleaming held by a score of clean pins
> I took till I see her hair again. (5)

As has been analysed in the earlier chapter, neither his father, mother nor his wife was able to provide him with a meaningful relationship. The mother is a recurring image in Ramanujan's poetry. The persona's present state of bewilderment and helplessness can be linked to the stiflingly conservative background of his mother.

In *The Striders*, there is one poem 'Still Another for Mother' which has the same theme of quiet despair. In the *puram* poems, there are six poems on 'Mothers' in the broad section entitled 'On Mothers.' In 'Mothers (1)' the mother is described as

> That dignified old woman
> with white hair
> that has given up
> all fragrant things,
> and withered breasts
> with nipples like eyes
> crinkled as the ironwood seed [32]

In 'Of mothers, among other things,' the mother's

> hands are a wet eagle's
> two black pink-crinkled feet
> one talon crippled in a garden
> trap set for a mouse. (61)

In 'Mothers (3)' the poet describes her thus

> The old woman's shoulders
>   were dry, unfleshed

with outstanding veins;
her low belly
was like a lotus pad.[33]

The point to be noted is that there appear to be a number of linguistic and imagistic parallels that evoke similar sentiments in these descriptions. Ramanujan evokes a mood through mere physical description. This is the 'enacting eye' for which he has been justly praised.

There is an ironic reversal of the mother's duties in 'Of Mothers, among other things.''A Mother's List of Duties' in the *puram* poem states:

To bring forth and rear a son is my duty
To make him noble is his father's . . .
To show him good ways is the King's
And to bear
A bright sword and do battle,
To butcher enemy elephants,
and come back.
that is the young man's duty.[34]

If the purpose is to locate thematic resonances then the poems on 'Mother' are an appropriate example. The son in 'Of Mothers, among other things' is neither responsible nor heroic. The mother had done her 'duty' by bearing and rearing him and in the process remained a symbol of 'domestic sterility,' but both the father and his tradition fail him. The 'young man' thus fails in his duty—both to his family and to his society.

The concentric circle of the poems now move outward to include interpersonal relationships. These relate to his wife and other relations. Society and self are interlinked in these poems. The same pattern of failure recurs in his domestic life, too. In the *Collected Poems*, there are three 'ironic' love poems addressed to his wife. The reason the poet gives for their emotional separation is 'unshared childhood.' These poems could be an adaptation of the *marutam* poems in the genre of *akam* poetry. The love that exists between them could be 'Kaikkilai' (unrequited love) or 'Peruntinai (mismatched love). The metaphoric landscape evoked in these poems is symbolic of incompatibility, sterility, and instability. Reference to places like Chicago, Alleppey and Kuwait (where the family was scattered) in *Love Poem for a Wife 1* symbolise modern rootlessness. The family is the unit of Indian culture. The disruption of the family indicates the breakup of this culture. The poet and his wife belonged to a culture that was deteriorating steadily. As mentioned earlier, *akam* poetry used the structural device of an inset which integrates the different elements of the poem and shapes its message. In *Love Poem for a Wife 2*, there is an ironic reference to the poem 'Self-Portrait.' Here the image of the mirror is deftly used to denote the incompatibility that existed between the persona and his wife.

But in the poem 'It Does Not Follow, But When in the Street,' the broken glass (another recurring image) is juxtaposed with the cascading yellow of the laburnum. The broken glass (another recurring image) symbolises the psychic disturbances which seek to expunge his personality. But the symbol of destruction is cancelled by the yellow flowers of spring, which are a symbol of hope. Images are juxtaposed in such a manner that they suggest a psychic rebirth. From this juxtaposition the poet arrives at a personal equation. In *akam* poetry, terms of comparison, whether implicit or explicit, are based on shape, color, action, result, touch, etc. Almost every image in Ramanujan's poetry can be studied in terms of various kinds of sense stimulation—such as visual, auditory, olfactory, gustatory, tactile and organic. The color of the yellow flowers, the imagined sharpness of the broken glass, and the resultant action of soaring optimism is another example of Ramanujan's dexterous use of structural and imagistic parallels.

In *The Black Hen*, there are a series of love poems entitled 'Love I: What she said,' 'Love 2: What he said, groping,' 'Love 3: What he said, remembering,' 'Love 4: What he said to his daughter,' 'Love 5' and 'Love 6: Winter.' These poems follow the structural pattern of the *akam* poems. Love here ranges from the personal to the objective; from obsession and uncertainty to the filial relationship between son and mother, father and daughter, and then to a lover's seeming boldness, and finally, to the soul's eternal longing for love. 'Love 6: Winter' ends thus:

> but unseeing, the eye within
> wants only red or green or grey,
> to sense in winter the heat,
> translate new signals in old
> ways, taking the dark for light. (233)

From the *akam,* the poet now moves on to the *puram*. The poet's background has so far been examined from the microcosm of the family. The social and cultural milieu to which the poet belonged has been analysed in detail in the previous chapter.

This background was as truncated and fragmented as the persona's own consciousness. Most of the poems in *The Black Hen* use stark images to evoke a mood of dread and fear.

In *Hymns for the Drowning* and *Speaking of Siva*, Ramanujan translated various Indian myths. In a series of poems in *The Black Hen* entitled 'Mythologies I,' 'Mythologies 2' and 'Mythologies 3,' the poet employs the technique of using Indian myths to articulate this fear.

In his translation of *bhakti* poetry, the only route to salvation is total surrender to God. This concept seems to have influenced him tremendously in his later years. *The Black Hen* offers a redemptive vision in spite of the disintegrating values of our times as is evident in the last poem entitled 'Fear No Fall.' There are innumerable references to Lord Murugan in his poetry. Lord Murugan is the Ancient Dravidan god of fertility, joy, youth, beauty, war and love. He is represented as a six-faced god with twelve hands. 'Prayers to Lord Murugan' in *Relations* has six sections. In the first section, Lord Murugan is greeted thus:

> Lord of the new arrivals
> lovers and rivals:
> arrive
> at once with cockfight and banner
> dance till on this and the next three

hills
Women's hands and the garlands
On the chests of men will turn like
chariot wheels. (113)

In 'A Guide to Lord Murukan,' "the guide poem and the heroic praise poem have become devotional. The subject is a god instead of a hero. The motifs, the landscapes, the moods of awe, love, and supplication, are directly in the classical Tamil heroic (puram) tradition. Murukan is both lover and chieftain. The interior (akam) and the exterior (puram), love and war, meet in him.[35]

In the Religious poems in *Poems on Love and War*, the poem 'Murukan: His Places' has remarkable parallels. When Lord Murukan arrives:

this cock-banner is raised
in the festival of festivals
for many towns around;
wherever devotees praise
and move His heart;
where his spear-bearing shamans
set up yards
for their frenzy dance.[36]

Eventually, the search for the Self which serves as the subjective centre of experience ends on a metaphysical and mystical note. It combines both the *Upanishads* and *bhakti* poetry with the Virashaiva tradition in Kannada, and the Shrivaishnava tradition in Tamil.

Though Ramanujan's poems are dominated by the twisted use of irony, yet a strain of the religious is discernible in his poems. In his choice of the works he chose to translate, it is remarkable that a poet so steeped in satire and cynicism, should deliberately, and with commitment translate two important volumes of devotional poetry, one in honour of Siva, and the other in praise of Vishnu.

Speaking of Siva is a book of *vacanas* in Kannada free verse. *Vacana* literally means 'saying, thing said.' In the *Vacanas*, the Virasaiva saints speak of Siva and speak to Siva. To the *bhakti* poets, true religion was the religion of the soul, unencumbered by dogmas and rituals. The *bhakti* poet was a visionary and a seer, a mystic of a high order. He was one who revealed his own self-realization so that others could transcend the limits of their finite self to attain a state of bliss. The *Vacanas* distinguished between *anubhava* 'experience,' and *anubhäva* (the Experience). *Anubhäva* is a search for the 'unmediated vision,' 'the unconditioned act,' 'the unpredictable experience.' [37] The emphasis was on 'the Experience,' a return to the primordial essence of Being itself, untrammeled by prayer, ritual and sacrificial offerings. Ramanujan observes, "Living in history, time, and cliché, one lives in a world of the pre-established, through the received *(Sruti)* and the remembered *(Smrti)*. But the Experience when it comes, comes like a storm to all such husks and labels."[38] The Virasaiva saints rejected both *Sruti* and *Smrti*. They were concerned with the experience of the Now. So their compositions were *Vacanas* or 'What is said.' It was concerned not with what was remembered or received, but with what was experienced now.

Mahadeviyakka is one of the poet-saints translated in this volume. Ramanujan does make a mention of her in his poem 'Mythologies 3.'

> 'Keep off when I worship Siva.
> Touch me three times, and you'll never
> See me again,' said Akka to her new groom
> who couldn't believe his ears. (228)

Mahadevi belonged to the twelfth century and was a contemporary of Basavanna. She was initiated into Siva worship at the age of ten. Legend has it that she fell in love with Siva as Mallikarjuna, translated either as 'the Lord White as Jasmine' or as 'Arjuna, Lord of goddess Mallika.' Most of her *Vacanas* end with the refrain 'O Lord White as Jasmine.' In her *Vacanas*, there is the essence of felt experience. Like Mira Bai, she was married in spirit to her Divine Lord. But worldly pressures led her to marry Kausika, or the chieftain of the land. However, she scorned all earthy obligations and affiliations, and set out 'wild and god-intoxicated' in search of her Lord. Her *Vacanas* record this search which follow all the phases of human love as exemplified in Sanskrit poetry. The three aspects of this love are 'love forbidden, love in separation, and love in union.' In her poems are found the traditional imagery of pan-Indian secular love poetry. The different phases of human love are metaphors for the different stages of mystic ascent. In her quest for divine ecstasy, she defies society, and subverts her role as a woman. She died into 'oneness with Siva' when she was barely in her twenties.

Bhakti involves a fullness of being in which the dualistic concept of Nara-Narayana, or I and Thou, blend into the One of the holistic consciousness. In the Vacanas, felt experience and creative expression fuse to engender a form of literature that is at once credible and enlightening. In effect, it would imply that reason can be transcended here leading to a redefinition of literary cognition and perception. Literary criticism should, therefore, include a level of critical perception that encompasses the motif of religious experiences as an acceptable norm of literary appreciation. Ramanujan's poem 'Fear No Fall' has subtle overtones of a greater insight, an intuitive power, and an extrasensory perception. In the last stage there is no worship anymore, "for who is out there to receive such worship? This is Oneness or *aikyasthala*. Like space joining space, water water, the devotee dissolves nameless in the Lord, who is not another."[39]

Hymns for the Drowning. Poems for Vishnu by Nammalvar have been translated from Tamil by A.K. Ramanujan. These poems are some of the earliest religious poems about Vishnu, or Tirumàl, the Dark one. There are twelve *alvars*, or saint-poets, devoted to Vishnu. These devotees of Vishnu, and their counterparts, the devotees of Siva (nayanmar), revitalized Hinduism between the sixth and ninth century. They followed the *bhakti* tradition, while checking the spread of Buddhism and Jainism. The poem 'Zoo Gardens Revisited' has remarkable parallels with the Vishnu portrayed in *Hymns for the Drowning.* In the last lines of this prose-poem the poet prays to Vishnu to protect all the birds and animals in the zoo which include flamingoes, ostriches, monkeys, orangutans, giraffes, tigresses, tigers and chimps from the cruelty and callousness of man. The poem appeals to the universal protector thus.

> Lord of lion face, boar snout, and fish eyes, killer of killer
> cranes, shepherd of rampant elephants, devour my lambs,
> devour them whole, save them in the zoo garden ark of your belly.
> (154)

In the poem 'The Man-Lion' taken from *Hymns for the Drowning*, Vishnu's manifestation in the form of the man-lion (Narasimha) is described.

> At the hour of sunset,
> there was blood
> on the heavens and the eight directions.
> Our lord
> plunged the demon into despair
> and slaughtered him:
> a lion
> tearing open
> a mountain under his claws.[40]

Hiranyakasipu, a king of the antigods, received a boon from Brahma that he should not be killed by weapons, thunderbolts, water, or fire; or by gods, demons, seers and other creatures created by Brahma; or in heaven, in earth, during the day or at night; neither from above, nor below. Vishnu took the form of a man-lion (Narasimha), who was neither man nor beast; took him on his knees—which was neither above or below; at sunset—which was neither day nor night; and disemboweled the demon with his claws—which were not weapons; on the threshold which was neither inside nor out.[41]

The 'lord of lion face' in the poem is obviously Narasimha. The 'boar snout' refers to Vishnu's third incarnation as a boar. In 'The Boar Rescues the Earth,' the Demon Hiranyaksa abducted the earth and kept it under the ocean. Vishnu became a boar, slew the demon after a thousand-year war and lifted the earth from the waters with his tusks.

> the seven islands of the earth,
> they stayed in place; . . .
> miraculously,
> that day
> our lord pitchforked them out
> with his tusks
> from the deep.[42]

Lord Vishnu also appeared as Matsya (fish eyes) who saved Manu, the ancestor of all human beings from the Great Flood. Manu was washing his hands when a fish came into his hands asking to be saved and promising to save Manu from a flood. With his tending, the fish outgrew every vessel, bank, and river till Manu carried it to the ocean (Vishnu the 'expander'). In the year the fish had indicated, Manu built a ship, tied its rope to the horn of the giant fish, which took him through the waters to the northern mountain. The flood swept away all other creatures.[43] This is described in 'Before I Could Say.'

> Before I could say,
> "He became cowherd
> fish
> wild boar,"
> he became a million million.[44]

'Cowherd' is Lord Krishna (another incarnation of Vishnu) and the wild boar also refers to a manifestation of Vishnu. The 'shepherd of rampant elephants' in Ramanujan's poem is a reference to the Indian myth where the Lord rushed to the rescue of Gajendra, the elephant, from the jaws of a powerful crocodile. The "Zoo garden ark of your belly" alludes to the Biblical story which tells us "that the almighty God saved two of every kind of creatures in Noah's ark when the entire creation was to be destroyed. . . . In this way," according to A.N. Dwivedi, "the poet has marvellously combined the Eastern and Western mythology in a harmonious whole, and thereby transcended the local for the universal and the familiar for the mythical."[45]

Another poem that can be analysed in a similar manner is 'The Difference.' Here:

> When Vishnu
> came to mind, the Dark one you know
> who began as a dwarf and rose in the world to measure
> heaven and earth with his paces. (172)

there is a reference to the poem 'He paces the worlds' where Vishnu 'The Dark one' as Vamana, the dwarf, measured the world in three steps.

The poem describes Vishnu and one of his works: how, as Vamana, he measured the worlds. Vishnu appeared as a dwarf, Vamana, before the demon King Bali who once ruled the world. The dwarf asked for a gift of a piece of earth three paces wide. Generous Bali gave him the gift. At once Vamana grew into gigantic Trivikrama, giant head and giant feet growing away from each other. He measured all earth in one stride, all heaven in another, and asked Bali where he could place his foot next. Bali, who saw that this figure was no other than Vishnu, bowed to him and asked him to place his foot on his (Bali's) head. Vishnu did so, and sent him to the nether-world. The name 'Vishnu' means "expander, pervader," and the myth probably refers to the process of creation.[46] In this comparative study, an attempt has been made to indicate affinity, tradition, and influence. A comparative study of Ramanujan's translation and his original poetic work affirms a contextualisation in terms of themes, motifs and structures. The influence of his translated works on his poetry has been assimilated to such a degree that one can speak of analogies and relational studies. The supreme critical act is not evaluation but recognition.

Indra Nath Chaudhari points out, "This kind of study leads us towards a broader idea of what literature is and raises different kinds of questions like noticing how literature manifests itself in different societies and circumstances."[47] Further analysis of his translation and poetry can perhaps yield more fruitful and startling parallels. Ramanujan's original poetry in English, to a large extent, has its roots in his translations. The sensibility is Indian, and it is couched in the Indian tradition. For this, he is indebted to his translations as a study of his poems reveal.

References

1. R. Parthasarathy, ed., *Ten Twentieth-Century Indian Poets* (Delhi: Oxford Univ. Press, 1976), p. 96.
2. Theodore Savory, *The Art of Translation* (London: Jonathan Cape, 1957), p. 42.
3. Samuel Johnson, "Alexander Pope (1688-1744)," *Lives of English Poets: A Selection* (London: Everyman's Library, 1979), p. 333.
4. Theodore Savory, 44.
5. "The Preface to Ovid's Epistles, translated by several hands," *John Dryden: Of Dramatic Poesy and other Critical Essays* (London Everyman's Library, 1962), p. 268.
6. Eugene A. Nida, *Language Structure and Translation* (Stanford: Stanford University Press, 1975), p. 33.
7. Sujit Mukherjee, *Translation as Discovery* (Hyderabad: Orient Longman, 1994), p. 9.
8. Mukherjee, p. 80.
9. Mukherjee, p. 8.
10. Mukherjee, p. 82.
11. Mukherjee, p. 82.
12. Mukherjee, pp. 82-83.
13. Mukherjee, p. 83.
14. "Translator's Note," *Poems of Love and War*. Selected and translated by A.K. Ramanujan. (Delhi: Oxford Univ. Press, 1985), p. xvii.
15. *Ibid.*
16. "Introduction," *Hymns for the Drowning*, trans. A.K. Ramanujan (Princeton: Princeton Univ. Press, 1981).
17. *Ibid.*, pp. xvi-xvii.
18. *Ibid.*, p. xvii.
19. *Poems of Love and War*, p. 297
20. 'Another Light on AKR,' Interview with Girish Karnad, *The Book Review*, N.D.
21. *Ibid.*
22. *Ibid.*

23. "Translator's Note," *The Interior Landscape*, trans. A.K. Ramanujan (London: Peter Owen, 1970), pp. 11-12.
24. *Poems of Love and War*, pp. xiv-xv.
25. *Interior Landscape*, pp. 105-6.
26. *Poems of Love and War*, p. 91.
27. *Ibid.*, p. 263.
28. *Ibid.*, p. 263.
29. Lachman M. Khubchandani, "The Bonds and Bounds of a Literary Tradition," *Comparative Literature*: *Theory and Practice*, ed. Amiya Dev, Sisir Kumar Das (Delhi: Allied, 1989), p. 107.
30. *The Collected Poems of A.K. Ramanujan* (Delhi: Oxford Univ. Press, 1995), p. xxxi.
31. *Poems of Love and War,* p. 163.
32. *Ibid.,* p. 180.
33. *Ibid.,* p. 182.
34. *Ibid.,* p. 185.
35. 'Afterword,' *Hymns for the Drowning. Poems for Vishnu* by Nammalvar, trans. from Tamil by A.K. Ramanujan (Penguin, 1992, 1993), p. 112.
36. *Poems of Love and War*, p. 215.
37. "Introduction" *Speaking of Siva*, trans. A.K. Ramanujan (New York: Penguin, 1973), p. 31.
38. *Ibid.*
39. *Ibid.,* p. 174.
40. *Hymns for the Drowning*, p. 9.
41. "Notes to the Poems," A.K. Ramanujan. *Hymns for the Drowning*, p. 89.
42. *Hymns for the Drowning*, p. 6.
43. "Notes to the Poems," A.K. Ramanujan, *Hymns for the Drowning*, p. 96.
44. *Hymns for the Drowning,* p. 49.
45. A.N. Dwivedi, *The Poetic Art of A.K. Ramanujan* (Delhi: B.R., 1995), p. 116.
46. "Notes to the Poems" A.K. Ramanujan, *Hymns for the Drowning*, pp. 87-88.
47. Indranath Choudhuri, *Comparative Indian Literature: Some Perspectives* (Delhi: Sterling, 1992), p. 5.

Conclusion:
Some Critical Observations

The critical scene in contemporary Indian English poetry is far from satisfactory. Very rarely, as one critic observed, is any difference made between criticism, reviews, and literary articles. However, from a survey of the developments in this field, it is evident that there has been a slow, though considerable, progress in the emergence of Indian English poetry as a disciplined and authentic genre of Indian writing in English. From being derivative and 'soulless,' Indian poetry in English has acquired a distinct voice of its own. No longer do Indian poets in English look to Western models for appropriation or assimilation. English, far from being a 'foreign language' or a 'second language,' has become to the urban educated Indian, a language that is as close to one's heart, if not closer, than one's mother-tongue. Many Indians who have been nurtured and educated in a Western-oriented environment, have readily accepted English as their first language. Whether this is to be derided or admired, only time will tell.

In fact, there have been many debates at seminars and conferences as to why an Indian should write in English when he has the potential of his own language to exploit, utilise, and enrich? Would he not be alienating himself from his own 'roots,' his tradition, and his culture by aligning himself with an 'alien tongue?' Ultimately, as a poet, shouldn't he be using an idiom that is native and central to his own self? In P. Lal's *Modern Indian English Poetry* (1969), certain basic issues about the poet's ability to use an alien language, their cultural isolation and confused identities, the uncertainty of critical authorities, and their bleak future, was discussed by the poets themselves.[1] To those critics of Indian poetry in English to whom English is an 'alien' language, Raja Rao's 1938 preface to *Kanthapura* provides an answer. "One has to convey in a language that is not one's own the spirit that is one's own. . . . English is not really an alien language to us. It is the language of our intellectual make-up-like Sanskrit or Persian was before—but not of our emotional make-up."[2] To the question whether Indian English poetry can be authentically or fully Indian, K.R. Srinivasa Iyengar states, "we want "Indianness" in our English, . . . but while some look for deposits of regional culture, others demand a whiff of the universal."[3] 'Universal' apparently referred to the broader spectrum of Indian thought and culture.

To Oliver Perry, "In post-colonial India contemporary Indian English poets have repeatedly been forced to deal with their 'Babu' image and attendant reputation as lackeys of British colonialism or of American neo-imperialism and/or 'new India's' elitist neo-colonialism. Still current is the narrow notion that they are inevitably alienated from India's national, regional, or pervasive folk cultures, as is shown by their choice of the non-indigenous English language and its implicit cultural, not to say, neo-colonial or imperialist, forms and values."[4]

But an analysis of A.K.Ramanujan's poetry proves otherwise. Of all his contemporaries, A.K. Ramanujan has the finesse and expert craftsmanship of an authentic creative writer. He does not lapse into romantic cliches or derivative models. His poems are remarkable for their deep emotion, and insights into the trauma of everyday existence. M.K. Naik observes, "His unfailing sense of rhythm gives a fitting answer to those who hold that complete inwardness with language is possible only to a poet writing in his mother tongue."[5] Though his earlier volumes of poetry dealt primarily with the social plane of experience, *The Black Hen* evokes subtle resonances of a metaphysical and spiritual reality.

From a thematic and imagistic analysis of his poetry in English, it is evident that Ramanujan's works deal with the psychic problem of adjustment between two cultures, the Indian and the

Western. The critical mode of enquiry adopted is that of psychoanalysis. Psychoanalysis is primarily a way of understanding man, and offering a possible 'cure' for his problems of maladjustment. The treatment aims to promote 'insight' or 'self-understanding,' and the 'cure' for which the patient seeks analysis is supposed to flow from this understanding. Such an understanding would involve confronting one's feelings and inclinations, and other dimensions of one's personality. When these are taken into account, then one can acquire a better appreciation of what one desires in the preoccupations and activities that fill one's life. A.K. Ramanujan's concern with his Indian past, his American present, and a return to his cultural roots through the mode of translations, reflect the quest of the Self for an inner world of stability and harmony. His translations of the religious Kannada *Vacanas* and the poems for Vishnu by Nammalvar reveal that the quest for inner quietude can perhaps be realised only through a spiritual reconciliation with his own Hindu heritage. His resort to the legend of the sinner/saint Arunagiri in 'Fear No Fall' is perhaps a testimony to the fact that ultimately in an age characterised by moral, intellectual and sexual decadence, a return to spirituality can liberate the self from the clutches of an ego-centric predicament.

The language of the unconscious is often expressed in the imaginative and symbolic use of language. The poetic imagination empowers one to transcend the limits of an egocentric and anthropocentric consciousness. This enables one to explore different possibilities of 'existence' which may be considered impossible at the level of established reality, but possible at a symbolic level. Alternative worlds of experience that were formerly repressed or unimagined are explored to engender a pluri-dimensionality of meaning. The poetics of the unconscious employs all linguistic and thematic deviations. The unconscious structures of language cannot be translated into the idioms of linear consciousness. Ramanujan's poetry constructs a poetics of the possible by positing things that can and should be changed. Reason and passion, intellect and emotion, logic and intuition are the two integral components of life itself. Each acts as a corrective over the excesses of the other. Without a judicious blend of these two elements, life itself would become sterile and meaningless. Acceptance of life would imply an acceptance of evil and suffering, disappointment and disillusionment, bitterness and cynicism. But this in turn could become redeeming if recycled constructively within the self. The redemptive vision of life would entail a tragic awareness of the contradictions of life, and an ability, through it, to experience and arrive at a higher level of perception and transcendent awareness. Ultimately, each individual is answerable for the meanings he finds or fails to find. In Ramanujan's poetry the cyclic process of the evolving self struggles towards a mode of coherence that is implicit in the myths and religious traditions of ancient India. The ritual of self-discovery leads the protagonist to a state where no questions are asked because no questions are needed. There is only the need to surrender one's self totally to a Divine being, and that moment of realisation is the persona's 'epiphanic' moment. To some cynics, such an interpretation might sound too reductionist. Had Ramanujan not died prematurely, maybe other interpretations of the poems he might have written later would have led to a different understanding of his works. But as things stand, such a reading appears to be the most plausible and the most credible. The truth of art lies in its power to inscribe new dimensions of reality. It is to this deeper reality that the spatio-temporal framework of Ramanujan's poetry leads to. The aesthetic content of his poetry is dependent on the symbolic and evocative power of words and images.

K. Ayyappa Paniker remarks, "A.K. Ramanujan is no true exile as long as he can translate from ancient Tamil or write about his grandfather or Murugan." He continues that A.K. Ramanujan writes with precision, detachment and objectivity, that at times reaches a rare degree of felicity both in poetic vision and in expression. "His wonderful agility and sureness of touch are the envy of even poets with English as their mother tongue. . . . Ramanujan is not poeticizing an alien experience. His poems escape from inauthenticity because of their avoidance of flamboyance and their controlled tone."[6]

Ramanujan's poetry is noted for its Indianness. His extensive knowledge of Kannada folklore enriched his poetic vision and interpretation. In his excellent essay on "Two Realms of Kannada Folklore," Ramanujan analyses the genre and system of the Kannada folklore. He argues that it "is a system where each genre is related to others, fitted, dovetailed, contrasted—so that we cannot study any of them alone for long."[7] For example, Kannada riddles complement Kannada proverbs in various ways. "The riddles have no social themes, as proverbs have. The riddles concentrate on familiar objects of nature (water, sun, eyes, trees, eggs etc.) or culture (well, book, sickle etc.) and play poetic and logical games with them."[8] A common Kannada riddle is: "What has three eyes but is not Siva?" The answer is 'A coconut .'

Proverbs on the contrary are used to illustrate a didactic point. In the example, "One bunch for the banana tree, one pregnancy for the scorpion," it is believed that a banana tree dies after one crop, and a scorpion dies after it gives birth to baby scorpions by bursting its back. These images are used to talk about any single and final deadly achievement. Proverbs are only used by adults, while riddles are used to entertain little children.

Proverbs and riddle complement each other in their universes of discourse as well as in their functions. Similarly, one may think of folk tale and myth, grandmother's tale and bardic narratives, ritual and theatre, non-literate traditions and literary ones as complementary context-sensitive parts of one system."[9]

Ramanujan further relates this domestic/public contrast to the ancient Dravidian categories of *akam* and *puram* as found in classical Tamil poetry.

A Flowering Tree and Other Oral Tales from India published posthumously in 1997 represent Ramanujan's oldest project. He began collecting tales for this book in the 1950s and continued to collect them till 1970. When he died in 1993, the translations of the tales were complete. But the brief introduction and the long, interpretive afterword that he planned to write were never completed. These fascinating folk tales of India reveal Ramanujan's passionate interest in all forms of folklore, though he was specially drawn to the folktale. Ramanujan's vast scholarship and insights represent a unique contribution to the study of the folktale in India. Stuart Blackburn and Alan Dundes, the editors of *A Flowering Tree* observe: "No other scholar in the twentieth century has fostered such a broad understanding of Indian culture among so many, and "no one could speak to him for five minutes without coming away with five new ideas."[10]

An analysis of Ramanujan's poetry, translations, and his rendering and interpretation of Indian folklore mark him as an extraordinarily gifted poet and artist. If poetry is an interpretation of life, then here is a man who through his art interpreted it richly, variously, and deeply.

The contemporary critical climate has witnessed the emergence of a number of 'younger' post-Ramanujan poets. If a more reliable poetic theory is to be postulated, it is necessary to have a balanced perception of both the earlier and later poets. It will be necessary to examine closely the role played by younger Indian poets in English in establishing a uniquely Indian poetic tradition. The process of assimilation of Western 'modernity' into Indian 'tradition' calls for careful scrutiny. The critical ideal would be to minimize as far as possible Western paradigms of intellectual enquiry, and to draw on modern Indian intellectual discourse. A significant development has been the emergence of women poets. Women poets like Eunice D'souza, Tejdeep, Imtiaz Dharker, Meena Alexander, Gauri Deshpande, Tillotama Rajan, Sujata Bhatt, and Melanie Silgardo are some of the poets who have managed to secure a place in this predominantly male-dominated sphere. Amongst the relatively 'younger' male poets, Vilas Sarang, Sharat Chandra, Sudeep Sen, Agha Shahid Ali, Vikram Seth, Sultan Padamsee, Ranjit Hoskote, Srinivas Rayaprol, and Hoshang Merchant have made significant contributions. Most of these poets divide their time between India and the

West. Their works have a commendable technical virtuosity, coupled with an acute insight into the dilemmas and anxieties of living in two worlds/cultures. Their poems acquire a transcultural context, where Indian tradition is juxtaposed with Western modernity. There also appears to be a post-modernist fluidity of history and hybridity. An interesting factor is that these poets consistently delve into their Indian tradition for novelty, modernity and meaning in their writings.

Vinay Dharwadker comments: "For the new poets and story tellers, the individual opportunities, family situations, social practices, economic and political conditions, and cultural institutions that constitute 'everyday reality' are radically different. Colonial India is as best a story, a discourse, an imagined or imaginary homeland, and the post-colonial India they know has barely begun to be charted. . . . In the course of the next twenty or thirty years they and their counterparts in the Indian languages functioning as both the sites and the instruments of a larger process of change, will once more alter our conceptions of what 'India' is and has been, of what is past, or passing, or to come."[11]

Most of these young poets have remained by and large unknown since their chances of entering the mainstream of Indian English poetry appear remote. The intellectual and stylistic innovations exemplified in their poetry call for a reassessment and re-evaluation of existing critical canons. An analysis of such a creative process can lead to fresh perceptions regarding the relationship between literature and society, the development of human imagination and intellect, the interaction between literature and the other arts. This, in fact, can lead to an eclectic approach towards the study of literature. A study of the trends and techniques can lead to further insights into the known cultural facets of Indian history such as eclecticism, multilingualism and multiculturalism. This can engender further studies in this field, thereby contributing to a definition of the modern Indian intellectual identity.

References

1. John Oliver Perry, *Absent Authority. Issues in Contemporary Indian English Criticism* (New Delhi: Sterling, 1992), p. 14.
2. *Ibid.*, p. 15.
3. *Ibid.*
4. *Ibid.*, p. 18.
5. M.K. Naik, *A History of Indian English Literature* (New Delhi: Sahitya Akademi, 1982), p. 201.
6. *Modern Indian Poetry in English*, ed. K. Ayyappa Paniker (New Delhi: Sahitya Akademi, 1991), pp. 17-18.
7. "Two Realms of Kannada Folklore," A.K. Ramanujan, *Another Harmony*, ed. Stuart H. Blackburn and A.K. Ramanujan (Delhi: Oxford Univ. Press, 1986), p. 41.
8. *Ibid.*
9. *Ibid.*, p. 42.
10. *A Flowering Tree and Other Oral Tales from India*, A.K. Ramanujan, ed. Stuart Blackburn and Alan Dundes (Penguin, 1997), p. x.
11. *The Oxford Anthology of Modern Indian Poetry*, ed. Vinay Dharwadker and A.K.Ramanujan (Delhi Oxford Univ. Press, 1994), p. 206.

Books in English by A.K. Ramanujan

Poetry

The Striders (1966).
Relations (1971).
Selected Poems (1976).
Second Sight (1986).

Translations

The Interior Landscape: *Love Poems from a Classical Tamil Anthology* (1967).

Samskara: *A Rite for a Dead Man*, a translation of U. Anantha Murthy's Kannada novel (1976).

Hymns for the Drowning. Poems for Vishnu by Nammalvar, trans. from Tamil (1981).

Poems of Love and War: From the Eight Anthologies and the Ten Long Poems of Classical Tamil (1985).

Folktales from India: *A Selection of Oral Tales from Twenty-two Languages* (1991).

Co-authored and Co-edited with Others

The Literatures of India: *An Introduction* (1975), with Edward C. Dimock, Jr., and others.

Another Harmony: *New Essays on the Folklore of India* (1986) with Stuart Blackburn.

When God is a Customer: *Telugu Courtesan Songs* by Ksetrayya and Others (1994), with V. Narayana Rao and David Shulman.

The Oxford Anthology of Modern Indian Poetry (1994), with Vinay Dharwadker.

Posthumous

The Black Hen in *The Collected Poems* (1994). *Collected Essays* (1995).

A Flowering Tree and Other Oral Tales from India. A.K. Ramanujan. Ed. Stuart Blackburn and Alan Dundes (1997).

Select Bibliography

Amanuddin, Syed. *World Poetry in English*: *Essays and Interviews.* New Delhi: Sterling, 1981.

Daruwalla, K.N., ed. *Two Decades of Indian Poetry*: *1960-1980*. New Delhi: Vikas, 1980.

Dwivedi, A.N. *Indo-Anglian Poetry.* 1979; Allahabad: Kitab Mahal, 1987.

______. *The Poetic Art of A.K. Ramanujan.*

______, ed. *Indian Poetry In English: An Anthology.* New Delhi: Arnold-Heinemann, 1980. New Delhi: B.R., 1995.

Gokak, V.K., ed. *The Golden Treasury of Indo-Anglian Poetry.* New Delhi: Sahitya Akademi, 1970.

______. *Studies in Indo-Anglian Poetry.* Bangalore: Sai Ratan Agency, 1972.

Iyengar, K.R. Srinivasa. *Indian Writing in English.* 1962; New Delhi: Sterling, 1984.

Jussawalla, Adil, ed. *New Writing in India.* Harmondsworth, Middlesex: Penguin, 1974.

Kulshrestha, Chirantan, ed. *Contemporary Indian-English Verse.* New Delhi: Arnold-Heinemann, 1980.

Lal, P., ed. *Modern Indian Poetry in English: An Anthology and a Credo.* Calcutta: Writers Workshop, 1969.

McCutchion, David. *Indian Writing in English: Critical Essays.* Calcutta: Writers Workshop, 1969.

Mohan, Ramesh, ed. *Indian Writing in English.* Madras: Orient Longman, 1978.

Naik, M.K. *Indian Response to Poetry in English.* Bombay: Macmillan, 1970.

____, ed. *Aspects of Indian Writing in English.* New Delhi: Macmillan, 1979.

____, ed. *Perspectives on Indian Poetry in English.* New Delhi: Abhinav, 1985.

Nandy, Pritish, ed. *Indian Poetry in English: 1947-72.* Calcutta: Oxford & IBH, 1972.

_____, ed. *Indian Poetry in English Today.* New Delhi: Sterling, 1973.

Narasimhaiah, C.D. *The Swan and the Eagle.* Shimla: The Indian Institute for Advanced Study, 1969.

Paniker, K. Ayyappa, ed. *Modern Indian Poetry in English.* New Delhi: Sahitya Akademi, 1991.

Parthasarathy, R., ed. *Ten Twentieth-Century Indian Poets.* Delhi: Oxford University Press, 1976

Peeradina, Saleem, ed. *Contemporary Indian Poetry in English.* 1972; Bombay: Macmillan, 1977.

Perry, John Oliver. *Absent Authority Issues in Contemporary Indian English Criticism.* New Delhi: Sterling, 1992.

Shahane, V.A. & Sivaramkrishna, M., ed. *Indian Poetry in English: A Critical Assessment.* New Delhi: Macmillan, 1980.

Walsh, William. *A Manifold Voice: Studies in Commonwealth Literature.* London: Chatto & Windus, 1970.